There Are Herbs in My Chocolate

by

Amber and Jacob Royer

Revised and Expanded Edition
Copyright 2019 Amber and Jake Royer

Contents

Preface
Specialized Equipment
Understanding Chocolate
Techniques For Working With Chocolate

Beverages

Chili-Spiced Hot Chocolate	20
Lavender and Roses Hot Chocolate	21
Fennel Espressino	22
The Bitter Chocolate	23
Lavender and Chocolate	24
Chocolate in the Afternoon	25
Thyme and Orange Hot Chocolate	26
Chocolate Rooibos Tea with Apricot and Hibiscus	27

Appetizers

Cocoa Balsamic Bruschetta	29
Grilled Sourdough with Chimichurri Dipping Sauce	30
Pineapple Salsa with Chocolate Tortilla Chips	32
Cheesy Cucumber and Dill Cups	34
Dark Chocolate Mushroom Arancini	36
Grilled Chicken Satay with White Chocolate Thai-Style Peanut Sauce	39
Sicilian-Style Meatballs with Cocoa Nibs	41

Brunch Dishes

Basil and Cocoa Breakfast Casserole	43
Chicken Chilaquiles with Cocoa Red Sauce	45
Grilled Vegetables with Cocoa Butter Pesto	47
Cocoa Balsamic Strawberry Spinach Salad	49
Cocoa Honey Fruit Salad	50
Chocolate Rosemary Pancakes with Strawberry Balsamic Syrup	51
Chocolate Chip, Pine Nut, and Basil Waffles with Orange Syrup	53
Hazelnut-Filled Tarragon Apple Crepes	55

Entrees

Fruit and Cocoa-Stuffed Pork Loin	58
Cocoa-Rubbed Skirt Steak with Gremolata	60

Chocolate BBQ Ribs	***62***
Black Mole Chicken	65
Chocolate Chili	69
Chocolate Coq au Vin	71
Lentil Stew with Cilantro Sour Cream Drizzle	74
Herbed Pumpkin Ravioli with Cocoa Brown Butter Sauce	75
Cheesy Pear and Chocolate Tortellini	77
Cocoa and Herb Fettuccine with Garlic Alfredo	79

Breads

Russian Black Bread	82
Pain au Chocolat a la Provence	84
Rosemary Honey Butter Roll with Dark Chocolate	89
Cranberry Sage and Blond Chocolate Beer Bread	91
Thyme and Pineapple Milk Chocolate Hawaiian Loaf	92
Fig and Fennel Chocolate Muffins	94

Ice Cream

Chocolate Mint and Matcha Ice Cream	96
Lavender Honey Ice Cream with Dark Chocolate Chunks	98
Cocoa Nib, Cinnamon and Bay Ice Cream	100
Blackberry and Sage Chocolate Gelato	101
Lemongrass White Chocolate Coconut Gelato	103

Cookies and Bars

Mint Chocolate Chip Cookies	106
Lavender Cocoa Nib Shortbread Cookies	107
Chocolate Lavender Madeleines	108
White Chocolate Coconut Lime Cookies with Cilantro	109
Thymely Chocolate Grapefruit Meringues	110
Chocolate Gingerbread	111
Ginger Mint Brownies	112

Cakes, Puddings and Pies

Chartreuse Black Forest Cake	115
Chocolate Cinnamon Cupcakes with Lemongrass Frosting	117
Rose Geranium Chocolate Pound Cake	119
Violet Chocolate Cheesecake	122
Chocolate Pear Tart with Herbed Sweet Dough Crust	124
Jasmine Liqueur Chocoflan	127
Lemon Verbena Chocolate Crème Brulee	129
Cocoa Masala Chai Soufflés	131

Espresso Tamarind White Chocolate Mousse
  with Clove Whipped Cream   133
Truffles and Candy
Gingered Ginseng Fudge   136
Hawaii-Inspired Mendiants   137
Rosemary Caramel-Filled Chocolates   138
Crystalized Ginger and Lemongrass Truffles   140
Pistachio and Cardamom Bark   143
**Pastes, Sugars,
Dressings and Syrups**

Preface

There is something about chocolate that awakens the imagination. From the samba beats of the Amazon rainforest where much of the world's raw cacao beans are harvested to the violin waltz of Vienna where chocolate desserts reached their pinnacle as an art form, chocolate has facilitated cultural connections within individual countries and around the globe. It has caused obsession, granted freedom (in London in the 1700s, chocolate houses were one of the few public places a "respectable" woman could go without a chaperone), and even led to a civilization's downfall. On November 4, 1519, Aztec Emperor Montezuma served Spanish conquistador Hernán Cortés a beverage made from cocoa and vanilla. Ten days later, Cortés took Montezuma hostage in his own palace, and in the end, the Aztecs wound up paying exorbitant "tribute" to the Spanish in the form of cocoa beans.

But what makes chocolate so special? Some would point to the caffeine content or that some studies suggest that theobromine increases production of serotonin in the brain. But we think it starts with the way chocolate feels in your mouth. It melts at body temperature, literally liquefying when it hits your tongue, which makes eating chocolate a sensory experience. Chocolate adds body and richness to other foods but can easily stand on its own.

A couple of years ago we were privileged to visit a cacao farm in the Dominican Republic. The experience really helped us to understand chocolate from a botanical perspective and helped spark the fascination that has resulted in this book as well as Amber's Chocoverse science fiction series.

Herbs and spices have been used to enhance chocolate since the Olmecs first started crushing cocoa beans into their drinks – before anyone ever thought of adding sweeteners. As chocolate traveled around the world, people enjoyed mixing local ingredients into their drinks, and later, after the innovation of solid chocolate, into their confections.

This book combines herbs and spices with chocolate, adding new elements to the flavors present in the chocolate. Each recipe offers a different flavor combination. Some are traditional combinations from various cultural kitchens; some are things that just happen to taste good together (at least to us and our taste testers: a rather informal group of friends and family). But if there is an herb you know you don't like, or something you'd just prefer to try, don't be shy about substituting one herb for another in any of these recipes.

We've included classic dishes that will supply you a full arsenal with which to show off your skills at manipulating chocolate. For instance, you will be able to bake a brownie, whip up a mousse, and roll a truffle. Once you have mastered the technique, we hope that you use the herbal components we've listed in any given recipe as an inspiration and springboard to your own herbal creations.

A few notes pertaining to all the recipes in this book:

All temperatures listed are in Fahrenheit.

Oven temperatures can vary, as can cooking times. You can use an oven thermometer to test the accuracy of your oven.

Mixer refers to a stand mixer. A large mixing bowl and hand-held mixer would work, too.

All recipes calling for butter use the unsalted variety.

Flour refers to unbleached all-purpose flour unless otherwise noted.

Sugar is granulated white cane sugar unless otherwise noted.

These recipes were tested with large size eggs.

As chocolate is a given in these recipes, the word "chocolate" may or may not appear in the title of a given recipe, but be assured that it is present.

All herbs should be fresh unless otherwise specified. Herbs should be harvested from a garden that does not use pesticides, or purchased from a reliable source. There are many inedible look-alike plants, so ask an expert if you need help identifying an herb.

Cautions When Using Herbs

Remember, not all herbs are appropriate for everyone. Be careful about possible interactions, especially if you are pregnant or taking prescription medications. It is also possible for a person to be allergic to a particular herb (just as with any food that a person may not have tried before). If you are uncertain if you or one of your dining guests should consume a particular herb, leave it out, substitute something you know is safe, or consult a medical professional. This book is not a substitute for proper medical advice, but is a celebration of the herbs that we enjoy in our own lives.

Specialized Equipment

Brulee Torch – These small hand-held torches can be used to melt sugar into caramel or to create browned surfaces on foods. If you don't have one, savory foods may be browned under a broiler, but do not attempt to do this with sugar. You are more likely to create a sticky mess than a brulee top.

Candy Molds – You can find candy molds in antique shops, thrift shops, or gourmet stores (especially if you are looking for high-tech silicone molds). However, the inexpensive molds you find at craft stores work just as well. If you don't have a mold, you could make round candies in a mini muffin tin.

Candy Thermometer – When you are tempering chocolate or making candy, a thermometer takes the guesswork out of the process. Some thermometers even have markings for "soft ball" and other candy stages.

Canning Jars – Make sure you use only actual canning jars. They are constructed to withstand high pressure and temperature. Do not reuse the jars from commercially packed grocery store foods as the glass may be thinner and more prone to breakage. Use new lids, and check to make sure there are no nicks in the sealant or in the edge of your jar.

Double Boiler – A double boiler (a two-part pan in which the top fits partially into the bottom) is almost required for working with chocolate, because it is so easy for the chocolate to burn when subjected to direct heat. If you don't have one, improvise one from a metal bowl that sits in the rim of one of your saucepans so that it will be over, rather than in, the simmering water.

Espresso/Cappuccino Machine – An actual espresso machine is required to get a nice crema on the top of your coffee. It also has an attachment for steaming and frothing milk. You can substitute strong coffee for the espresso in recipes, but to make Italian-style coffee beverages, the machine is a must. If you don't have one, go for the more laid back French café au lait, where you can infuse herbal flavors into the warm milk before you add it to the coffee.

Food Mill – This is a hand-cranked machine that allows you to separate liquid and pulp from food solids. It usually comes with three different-sized blades, depending on how finely you need the food processed. If you don't have one, you can use the back of a wooden spoon and a sieve. There is a conical-shaped French-style sieve (chinois) specifically designed for straining stock and eliminating seeds and other solids from foods.

Ice Cream Maker – There are a variety of styles of home ice cream maker. We prefer the old-fashioned kind where you add rock salt and ice. Some of the other designs don't seem to get cold enough to make proper ice cream. If you don't have an ice cream maker, pour the ice cream mix into a wide metal pan and place in the freezer, stirring the mixture every half hour or so. Keep in mind that still-frozen ice cream won't be as creamy as the churned varietay and may be slightly gritty.

Madeleine Pan – This pan has individual molds for small seashell-shaped cakes. They come in a standard size and a miniature (bite size) variation. They are traditionally used to make French butter cakes of the same name but could be used to mold other foods.

Molinillo – This is a traditional wooden whisk used for frothing chocolate. They can be quite decorative but are usually inexpensive. If you don't have one, you can put the hot chocolate mixture in a blender, but be careful removing the lid, as steam coming out of the blender cup can be quite hot.

Mortar and Pestle – These cup-shaped vessels are used for hand-grinding foods into powders and pastes. You may find a spice grinder for powders and a food processor for pastes much more efficient. If you don't have any of these, mince your ingredients as finely as possible with a sharp knife.

Pasta Machine – A pasta machine makes it easy to roll out uniform sheets of pasta and to cut the sheets into noodle shapes. It takes a little bit of practice to do this without tearing the sheets, but it is a time saver in the long run. In lieu of a pasta machine, you can use a rolling pin and a sharp knife.

Pastry Bag – While pastry bags are not strictly necessary for creating any of the recipes, they do assist in transferring foods neatly and in creating a decorative presentation. The decorative tips suggested for use are round and star tips in medium and large sizes.

Scale – A kitchen scale is handy for weighing the chocolate. We prefer the digital type. Try to find one that will let you put any bowl on it to prevent having to clean the built-in bowl in the middle of steps.

Spice Grinder – A spice grinder quickly and easily processes whole spices into powder. If you don't have one, grind your spices in a mortar and pestle. If you don't have one of those either, and the ingredients are not soft enough to mince with a knife, then place the spices in a zipper bag and pound them with the flat side of a meat tenderizer (although you will probably find that some pieces are not as well crushed as you would like).

Springform Pan – This is a pan that comes in two pieces: a base that the food sits on and a ring or collar that has a closure that can be sprung open, allowing the ring to be removed easily. It is very difficult to get a clean edge on foods such as cheesecakes without one.

Tea Ball – Tea balls are little enclosures for loose tea leaves. You can also use them to hold herbs and spices that you want to add to a cooking liquid and later remove. If you don't have a tea ball, strain tea after brewing or tie herbs up in a piece of cheesecloth or a coffee filter.

Understanding Chocolate

Cocoa Content

Chocolate bars often have a number followed by a percent sign printed prominently on the package. This number tells you the ratio of cocoa mass (solids that come directly from the cocoa bean, plus any additional cocoa butter) to other ingredients. Simply put, the higher the percentage number, the less sweet the chocolate. Keep in mind that this does not necessarily correspond to the level of perceived chocolatey taste, which has a lot to do with the quality of the beans and how they are processed. It is also not a judgment of quality.

Types of Chocolate

Unsweetened Chocolate – Pure chocolate liqueur (the liquid form of cocoa mass) that has been hardened into blocks. This is also known as bitter chocolate or baking chocolate.

Dark Chocolate – European standards require dark chocolate to have a minimum of 35% cocoa solids. The FDA uses that same number as the minimum requirement for a product labeled "semi-sweet" or "bittersweet." These chocolates also must have less than 12% milk solids. Anything above 12% is considered "milk chocolate." While one company's bittersweet may have the same percentage as another's semisweet, here are the rough definitions:

> *Bittersweet Chocolate* – Typically contains about of its weight as sugar. Usually refers to bars in the 65 - 85% range. However, this labeling is not regulated and is completely up to discretion of the manufacturer.
>
> *Semisweet Chocolate* – Typically contains about ½ of its weight as sugar. Usually refers to bars in the 35 - 60% range. However, this labeling is not regulated and is, again, completely under the purview of the manufacturer.

Sweet Chocolate – In order for a substance to be called "chocolate," the FDA requires that it contain at least 15% chocolate liquor. So, sweet chocolate ranges from 15%, until you hit semisweet.

Milk Chocolate – The FDA requires chocolates labeled as "milk chocolate" to contain at least 10% chocolate liqueur and a minimum of 12% milk solids. The European standard for milk chocolate is similar but requires a minimum of 25% milk solids. British chocolates more often use a base of powdered milk, whereas US milk chocolates are often based on condensed milk, giving the two products a very different flavor.

White Chocolate – This confection is made with cocoa butter rather than cocoa solids, which accounts for its creamy taste and pale color. Check the label carefully to ensure you are getting genuine white chocolate, which, according to the FDA must contain at least 20% cocoa powder and 14% milk solids. Inferior "white chocolate" substitutes vegetable oil for the cocoa butter, rendering it chocolate-free. Chocolate that is paper-white in color has been subjected to a deodorizing treatment which removes all traces of cocoa solids – and all of the unique character. There are a few companies making non-deodorized white chocolate, which is ivory or light brown.

Blond Chocolate – This is white chocolate that has been caramelized to create a product similar to dulce de leche. Some prefer it because it tones down the intense sweetness of white chocolate.

Stone-Ground Chocolate – Cacao is grown in a band randing 20° north and south of the equator. Refrigeration is not common in these areas, which is why chocolate processed there is usually grainy and primarily made into beverages. It is typically grated for use.

Stone ground chocolate

Artisanal Chocolate Makers

The best thing about artisanal chocolate makers is their passion for the subject – and their ingenuity. We've attended presentations where these entrepreneurs describe winnowing cocoa beans with a hairdryer or figuring out how to keep a second-hand chocolate conch (the machine used for "massaging" chocolate to make it smooth, with a pleasant mouthfeel) running. They are championing quality and innovation and sometimes involve themselves in the entire chocolate-making process, from visiting the countries where the beans are grown to negotiate directly with the farmers to marketing the finished bar. Artisanal chocolate commands a premium price but keep in mind that these small operations not only have more overhead but are more likely to be supporting fair trade for the cacao farmers. The great thing is that there are now so many different artisanal companies with different styles and philosophies of chocolate, you are bound find something you like.

For baking and dessert making, however, you may find mass-produced chocolate more reliable, as the flavors will have a more uniform taste.

Single-Source Chocolate

Flavors developed in single-source cacao beans depend not only in the area where it is grown, but on soil and growing conditions. This means that the taste of a certain bean may vary from year to year (in a manner similar to wine). This makes it difficult for chocolate makers to create a consistent product, which is why most large manufacturers use a blend of beans, and single-source chocolates are usually the territory of artisanal chocolate makers. This same lack of consistency – and the distinctiveness of flavors – can be problematic when using single-source chocolates in recipes designed for blended chocolates. You will need to take into account such nuances when matching flavors and adjusting amounts of sweeteners.

Where Does Chocolate Come From?

Green cacao pod on tree

Chocolate is made from seeds of the theobroma cacao, a tropical tree that produces football-shaped pods that vary in color from yellow to red (brown or black pods are a sign of disease). The beautiful cacao flowers are cauliflorous, meaning they grow on flower pads that form on the limbs and trunk of the tree instead of at the end of stems. The pods must be cut from the tree rather than pulled off, as pulling destroys the flower pads, which the tree cannot replace. This is a labor-intensive process that usually involves a machete. One pod contains an average of 40 seeds (cacao beans), and a tree may produce 20 – 30 pods in a year. It takes roughly 400 beans (or 10 pods) to create a pound of dark chocolate.

Originally, people ate the pulp (which tastes a little like a cross between pineapple and sour candy) and discarded the seeds. This is because the seeds are quite unpalatable until they are processed, which takes place in several steps.

The beans and pulp are placed in a box where they are allowed to ferment for about a week, busily developing flavors. Then, after the fermented pulp has drained away, the beans are dried, roasted, and then have their outer hulls removed. At this point, the beans are coarsely ground into nutty-tasting pieces called nibs.
Some people like to snack on cocoa nibs to get their chocolate fix while consuming relatively few calories. Nibs also make a flavorful substitute for chocolate chips in baking recipes. You can purchase nibs by the bag in reasonable quantities.

To continue the processing, nibs are further ground into a thick paste or viscous liquid known either as "chocolate mass" or "chocolate liquor."

To make cocoa powder, the liquor is pressed, taking the cocoa butter content down from just over half to somewhere closer to 15%. Alkali is often added to mellow the flavor in a process known as Dutching. An alternative method known as the Broma process involves hanging the mass in a heated room and allowing the cocoa butter to drip off, producing a drier powder. Natural and Dutched cocoa powders have very different flavor profiles, and the differences in the acidity levels can affect how they interact with leaveners when baking.

Nibs being ground by hand

To make unsweetened chocolate, the chocolate liquor is finished as is. For dark chocolate, the chocolate liquor is ground together with the desired percentage of sugar and vanilla. In order to make milk chocolate, milk solids or condensed milk is added. The mix of cocoa and milk is often dried into a taffy-like texture called chocolate crumb. Extra cocoa butter is usually added to the crumb.

Chocolate intended for eating out of hand, for candy making, or to be formed into baking bars are then "conched" in a large rotating machine that kneads and massages the chocolate until it is smooth. This can take from 4-72 hours depending on the desired quality of the chocolate and the ingredients included in it.

Chocolate must be tempered to give it that "snap" when you break the bar and to keep it from becoming gritty. To do this, the chocolate is heated and then cooled in such a way that it crystallizes properly. The chocolate you buy for home use is usually already tempered. In order to use it to make confections, you will need to melt it and then re-temper it. We have provided instructions for doing so **(see page 17)**.

Finally, the chocolate is formed into bars or molded into other shapes.

Broken chocolate

Techniques For Working With Chocolate

Storing Chocolate

Store chocolate in a cool, dry place, preferably between 62 and 70° fahrenheit. Keep chocolate well wrapped, and do not store with aromatic foods, as it can absorb odors.

Chocolate can be refrigerated if the weather necessitates, but it tends to bloom (create a whitish speckled appearance wherein the sugar has started to crystalize due to excess humidity). The opposite problem (a streaky-appearing bloom created when the fat starts to separate) occurs when chocolate gets too warm and is not subsequently tempered. Bloomed chocolate is still edible, just not attractive, and can be easily melted into recipes.

Chocolate can be frozen, but it should be wrapped exceptionally well (airtight, in foil, inside an airtight zipper bag) to prevent humidity, and it should be thawed slowly: first in the refrigerator and then on the counter. Thaw completely before opening the bag.

Chopping Chocolate

To cut chocolate for easy melting, choose a long, serrated knife and cut across the bias of the chocolate (on a diagonal to the square or rectangular shape). Turn the block and work evenly across all four corners.

If you prefer, you can purchase pistols (small disks of pure chocolate), which are made to be melted without any need for chopping. These are not the same as chocolate chips, which are intended to keep their shape during the cooking process. Chocolate chips should not be substituted for bar chocolate.

To cut chocolate into chunks, use a chef's knife. You can also use a chef's knife to make chocolate curls. Position a large block of chocolate so that it is stable. Hold the knife with both hands at a slant towards you, and press down on the chocolate block, shaving curls as you pull the knife carefully towards you.

Melting Chocolate

It is very easy to scorch chocolate when melting it. There is no way to repair burnt chocolate, so be careful.

This problem can be minimized by using a double boiler over barely simmering water rather than placing a pan filled with chocolate over direct heat. Be careful not to splatter any water into the chocolate, which can cause it to seize (dry particles – cocoa and sugar – in the chocolate become moist and form a gritty, rough mess).

All ingredients added to melted chocolate should be at room temperature or should be tempered by adding small amounts of the warmer ingredient into the cooler ingredient to bring up the temperature while whisking constantly. This prevents the chocolate from being shocked and becoming separated or lumpy.

If you find yourself having to melt chocolate in a microwave, make sure to stir at 10-15 second intervals. Don't try to determine if it's melted visually. Chocolate can hold its shape while it is burning inside.

Salvaging Seized Chocolate

If you are planning to use the chocolate with other ingredients, as in a chocolate beverage or brownie batter, you can add boiling water a tablespoon at a time to smooth out the seized chocolate. However, you cannot use melted seized chocolate for any recipe requiring tempering.

Tempering Chocolate

Chocolate needs to be re-tempered after melting to ensure that it doesn't melt at room temperature or fall apart when filled or molded.

To Temper Dark Chocolate: Chop the chocolate. Heat half of it in a double boiler over barely simmering water. Stir until the chocolate's temperature reads between 115 and 120° on a candy thermometer (the chocolate will melt quickly and may come to temperature before all the chocolate is melted). Remove the saucepan from the heat and stir until the chocolate is melted through and smooth. Add the rest of the chocolate in batches until it is all incorporated. Adding the chocolate in this method will "seed" the chocolate with crystals and make sure it tempers correctly. Stir continually. When the chocolate starts to thicken, check the temperature again. Keep stirring until the temperature drops to less than 90°. At this point it is tempered and you can use it as such.

To test whether it's tempered you can dip a knife into it and put the knife in the fridge for a few minutes. The sample should harden well. Milk chocolate and white chocolate temper at between 86 and 88°.

Beverages

In this Chapter you will find:

Chili-Spiced Hot Chocolate

Lavender and Roses Hot Chocolate

Fennel Espressino

The Bitter Chocolate

Lavender and Chocolate

Chocolate in the Afternoon

Thyme and Orange Hot Chocolate

Chocolate Rooibos Tea with Apricot and Hibiscus

Chili-Spiced Hot Chocolate

Makes 2 Servings

Cacao was first cultivated by the Mayans and the Aztecs. It was so revered in Aztec culture that xocolatl (sometimes spelled "chocolatl"), the unsweetened cocoa drink flavored with chilies or vanilla, was reserved for royalty, priests and decorated soldiers. A commoner caught drinking this forbidden liquid faced stoning or death as a human sacrifice. The Aztecs were considered the most outstanding herbalists of their day (the few surviving codexes list nearly 3,000 herbs used in medicinal or culinary preparations), so we consider it authentic to add epazote (an herb used in South Mexican and Guatemalan cuisine and medicine) for a unique taste. Epazote has notes of has notes of oregano, anise, citrus and mint.

Achiote, also known as annatto, is traditionally used to deepen the color of chocolate and to give it an earthy flavor. This beverage would not have originally contained dairy or sweetener, but feel free to use them if you are not a fan of bitter flavors. Honey would have been available in the era before sugar cane came to the Americas and would thus be a good choice as your sweetener.

2 cups water (or milk)
3-4 epazote leaves
6 ounces tablet-style stone-ground chocolate, grated
½ teaspoon canella (white cinnamon), plus additional for garnish
½ teaspoon allspice
½ teaspoon cayenne pepper
1 teaspoon achiote (annatto)
¼ teaspoon salt
¼ cup honey

Heat the water in a medium saucepan just until it reaches a simmer. Turn off the heat and add the epazote leaves. Allow the leaves to steep for 10-15 minutes, then remove and discard leaves. Return the saucepan to the heat and bring the liquid back to a simmer. Add the grated chocolate, whisking constantly until it melts and the mixture becomes smooth. Remove the saucepan from the heat and add the canella, allspice, cayenne pepper, achiote, and salt. Sweeten with the honey, if desired. Immediately before serving, froth the beverage with a molinillo. Serve garnished with a dash of cinnamon.

Lavender and Roses Hot Chocolate

Makes 8 Servings

This is the technique for making a Parisian style le chocolat chaud: a rich, thick hot chocolate that borders on becoming a drinkable ganache. You will notice that there isn't any added sweetener. The real flavor here comes from using a high-quality chocolate with a taste profile you enjoy, so don't skimp on your choice. This beverage has a very French feel to it, as it stars the floral herbs that are indicative of France. Lavender's connection to Provence is obvious, but what of the roses? Josephine (as in Napoleon and Josephine) had a serious passion for roses. Her house, Château de Malmaison, was once the site of one of the most extensive rose gardens ever created. Her aspiration was to include a specimen from all known rose varieties, and Napoleon even ignored maritime law when she had his warship commanders search all seized vessels for viable rose plants and seeds.

1 cup heavy cream
8 ounces bittersweet chocolate, chopped
3 tablespoons food-grade lavender flowers
2 tablespoons food-grade rosebuds

Per Serving:
¼ cup milk
¼ teaspoon vanilla

In a medium saucepan, bring the cream, lavender flowers and rosebuds to a rolling boil. Immediately remove the saucepan from the heat, and allow the mixture to steep for at least 20 minutes. Strain out the flowers and whisk in the chocolate (return the saucepan to a low heat if necessary to melt the chocolate through). Strain the mixture through a fine-mesh sieve, pushing it through with a rubber spatula. Refrigerate the chocolate concentrate in a covered jar for up to 10 days.

For each cup of hot chocolate, stir together ¼ cup chocolate concentrate and ¼ cup milk in a small saucepan over low heat. Stir constantly until the mixture is warmed through but not boiling. Stir in the vanilla, pour the hot chocolate into a mug, and serve immediately.

Fennel Espressino

Makes 2 Servings

In Italy, a cappuccino or cioccolata calda is often all a person has for breakfast (there may sometimes be a croissant involved as well). If that feels like too much sugar in the morning, opt for an espressino instead. It's like a miniature cappuccino served in an espresso cup with cocoa powder both in the bottom of the cup and on the top. Milk-based coffee beverages like this one are typically done with by about 10:00 in the morning in Italy, when tradition dictates you switch to espresso and that you call it "un caffe." Fennel is native to the Mediterranean, and brewing the finely ground seeds will lend an interesting licorice element to the coffee itself. This is intensified by the fennel-infused syrup. The amount used is very small. Use 2% milk for more froth volume and for easier pouring.

4 teaspoons cocoa powder
Espresso-grind coffee, measured to fit your machine
1 tablespoon fennel seeds, finely ground
1 teaspoon fennel-Simple Syrup (see page 151)
¼ cup cold milk, for steaming

Sprinkle 1 teaspoon of the cocoa powder in the bottom of each of two espresso cups. Mix the ground fennel seeds with the ground coffee and pack into a cappuccino machine. Pull two espresso shots according to the manufacturer's directions. Immediately pour the shots into the espresso cups. Add ½ teaspoon of the fennel syrup to each cup and top with the remaining cocoa powder. Pour the milk into a frothing pitcher. Froth the milk using the machine's steam wand, heating the milk to between 150-155°. Make sure you keep the wand at least a few centimeters under the surface of the milk, moving it deep inside the milk and turning the pitcher as the heat builds. Swirl the frothed milk in the pitcher for a few seconds. If you see bubbles, pound the pitcher on a countertop a couple of times, then swirl again. Pour the milk froth slowly into the cup, moving the pitcher from side to side until the desired pattern emerges (you will not use all the milk). Serve immediately.

The Bitter Chocolate

Makes 1 Serving

Angostura Bitters, a concentrated herbal alcoholic preparation, is used in a number of classic cocktails, including the aptly named, "Old Fashioned." It can easily overwhelm the other flavors in a drink, and in this one, you want to be able to taste both the orange and the chocolate, so use a light touch. If you have the time, making your own cherries using Maraschino liquor will help you top off this drink without fluorescent colors ruining the sophisticated vibe.

The bitters were first produced in the town of Angostura (now Ciudad Bolívar, Venezuela). The concoction does not, however, contain angostura bark. 'Angostura' is Spanish for 'narrowing.' This feels appropriate because the town of Angostura was located at the first narrowing of the Orinoco River. Like most herbal liqueurs, Bitters were developed as a health tonic, this one by Johann Gottlieb Benjamin Siegert), surgeon general in Simón Bolívar's army in Venezuela in the 1800s.

Ice
5 oz. orange juice
2 oz. vodka
2 oz. Crème de Cacao
¼ oz. Bitters
Maraschino Cherries, for garnish (see page 23)

Fill a highball glass partway with ice. Add the orange juice, vodka, Crème de Cacao and Bitters and stir to combine. Thread several Maraschino cherries onto a short skewer and balance across the top of the glass.

Lavender and Chocolate

Makes 1 Serving

The lavender simple syrup in this drink is subtle, but it gives the ice-cream based cocktail a whole other dimension. Make sure to crush the ice before adding the other ingredients, so that you don't wind up with chunks of ice ruining the texture of the drink.

1 c. crushed ice
2 scoops chocolate ice cream
1 oz. chocolate syrup
4 oz. lavender-**Simple Syrup** (see page 151)
1 oz. Crème de Cacao
¼ c. whipped cream
lavender flowers, for garnish

Combine the ice, ice cream, both syrups, and the Crème de Cacao in a blender and pulse until smooth. Pour into a glass, and top with the whipped cream. Sprinkle on 3 or 4 lavender flowers for garnish.

Maraschino Cherries

¾ c. granulated sugar
¾ c. ginseng green tea (prepared)
¼ c. lemon juice
1 cinnamon stick
½ tsp. freshly grated nutmeg
1 tbsp. vanilla extract
1 ½ lb. sweet cherries, pitted
1 ½ c. Maraschino liqueur

In a large pot over medium-high heat, combine the sugar, ginseng green tea, lemon juice, cinnamon stick, nutmeg and vanilla. Bring the mixture to a boil, the reduce the heat to medium-low. Add the cherries and simmer for around 7 minutes. Remove from the heat and stir in the Maraschino liqueur. Store in the refrigerator for at least a week before eating.

Chocolate in the Afternoon
Makes 1 Serving

In Italy, a cappuccino or cioccolata calda is often all a person has Ernest Hemingway was once asked to submit a recipe to a cookbook wanting contributions from famous writers. His response was to invent Death in the Afternoon, a cocktail composed of 1 ½ oz. Absinth, topped with champagne. This cocktail is a bit less intense, but you can still feel very literary and elegant drinking it.

1 oz. Crème de Cacao
½ oz. Absinth (or other herbal liquor)
champagne, chilled

Pour the Creme de Cacao and Absinth into a champagne flute. Top with champagne to fill the glass.

Thyme and Orange Hot Chocolate

Makes 2 Servings

This hot chocolate is our tribute to the Terry's Chocolate Orange. When we were kids, a chocolate orange (yes, the kind that directed you to "Whack and Unwrap") was a rare treat. Terry's has included real orange oil in their chocolate oranges since they first introduced them in 1931. In order to get the most orange oil out of the peel, make sure you use a fresh orange and that you zest it right into the pot. The lemon thyme leaves supply a supporting citrus flavor.

¾ cup milk
¾ cup half and half
3 tablespoons brown sugar
1 tablespoon orange zest
2 teaspoons lemon thyme leaves
4 ½ ounces milk chocolate, broken into pieces
Orange wedges, for garnish

In a small saucepan, combine the milk, half and half, brown sugar, orange zest and lemon thyme over medium-low heat. Cook, stirring frequently, until the mixture comes to a simmer. Simmer for 2 minutes, but do not let the mixture boil. Remove the saucepan from the heat, cover and allow the liquid to steep for at least 10 minutes. Place the chocolate in a large bowl. Strain the liquid into the bowl, discarding zest and leaves. Whisk until the chocolate is melted through. Serve in a mug garnished with an orange wedge.

Chocolate Rooibos Tea with Apricot and Hibiscus

Makes 6-8 Servings

If you need a healthier way to get your chocolate fix, consider steeping cocoa nibs in a tisane. Red rooibos (sometimes known as bush tea) is a member of the legume family that grows in a small belt of the western cape of South Africa. It has linear, needle-like leaves with a natural caramelly, sweet flavor that reduces or eliminates the need to add additional sweeteners to tisaines brewed from it. South Africa also has a Hibiscus Coast, where visitors can enjoy the plentiful hibiscus flowers, which are great for teas because they provide a citrus note and a fruitiness reminiscent of cranberries. We've included them here along with apricots, a common element in African cooking that adds an even sweeter note. This mixture also makes for a refreshing iced tisane.

2 tablespoons cocoa nibs
¼ cup red rooibos
1 tablespoon dried hibiscus flowers, crumbled
2 tablespoons dried apricots, diced

Combine all ingredients in a container that has an airtight lid. To brew tea, warm a personal-sized teapot with a little water and discard. Add 8 ounces of boiling water to the teapot. Fill a tea ball halfway with the rooibos mixture (approximately 1 ½ teaspoons). Allow to steep for 3-4 minutes, then pour into a warmed teacup and serve immediately.

Herbie Info Box

Hibiscus flowers sold for tea are sometimes labeled "sorrel." This should not be confused with garden sorrel, which is cultivated for its leaves.

Appetizers

In this Chapter you will find:

Cocoa Balsamic Bruschetta

Grilled Sourdough
with Chimichurri Dipping Sauce

White Chocolate Sourdough

Pineapple Salsa
with Chocolate Tortilla Chips

Chocolate Tortilla Chips

Cheesy Cucumber and Dill Cups

Dark Chocolate Mushroom Arancini

Dark Chocolate Mushroom Risotto

Grilled Chicken Satay
with White Chocolate Thai-Style Peanut Sauce

Sicilian-Style Meatballs
with Cocoa Nibs

Cocoa Balsamic Bruschetta

Makes 4 Servings

This is one of our favorite uses for chocolate-infused balsamic, which adds a rich, luscious tang to the simple tomato preparation. The undernotes in balsamic include caramel and wine, which makes sense given that it is usually made from cooked grape must (freshly crushed grape juice with all the skins, seeds and stems). It originated in Italy, where the name implied "balsam-like" in the sense of "restorative" or "curative." We've paired it here with fresh Italian staples: tomatoes, basil and mozzarella. What could taste more like summer? Brushing the toasts with melted cocoa butter reinforces the chocolate taste and adds a nutty element to the dish.

3 ½ cups ripe plum tomatoes, diced
2 garlic cloves, minced
1 tablespoon olive oil
2 tablespoons chocolate-infused balsamic vinegar
6-8 fresh basil leaves, chopped
1 teaspoon salt
1 teaspoon black pepper
1 baguette or other long, thin bread
¼ cup cocoa butter, melted
½ cup fresh mozzarella, crumbled

Preheat oven to 450°.

Put tomatoes, garlic, olive oil, chocolate-infused balsamic, basil, salt and pepper in a bowl and mix gently. Set aside.

Slice the baguette on a diagonal into ½-inch thick slices. Use a pastry brush to coat one side of each slice with cocoa butter. Place on a baking sheet, cocoa butter side down. Put the baking sheet in the oven. Bake for 5-6 minutes, until the bread just begins to turn golden brown.

Place the warm crostini cocoa-butter side up on a serving tray and top each toast with a spoonful of the bruschetta mixture and a few bits of mozzarella.

Grilled Sourdough with Chimichurri Dipping Sauce

Makes 6-8 Servings

Grilled bread with chimichurri is a traditional appetizer in Argentina, where the same sauce is often served on grilled meats. You need a flavorful bread to stand up to the intense tang of the chimichurri. Serve while the bread is still warm from the oven.

1 loaf White Chocolate Sourdough (see page 30)
Olive oil, for brushing
2 cups fresh flat-leaf parsley leaves, hard packed
5 garlic cloves
1 teaspoon salt
½ teaspoon black pepper
½ teaspoon red pepper flakes
½ teaspoon dried oregano
½ cup olive oil
¼ cup red wine vinegar
¼ cup lemon juice
1 tablespoon lemon zest

Preheat oven to 450°.

Combine the parsley leaves, garlic cloves, salt, pepper, red pepper flakes, oregano, olive oil, red wine vinegar, lemon juice and lemon zest in a food processor or blender. Pulse on high until pureed.

Slice the loaf on a diagonal into ½-inch thick slices. Use a pastry brush to coat both sides of each slice with olive oil. Place on a baking sheet. Put the baking sheet in the oven. Bake for 3 minutes, and then flip the bread and continue toasting another 2-3 minutes until the bread just begins to turn golden brown.

Serve the chimichurri in a bowl alongside the toasted bread.

White Chocolate Sourdough

½ cup fed **Sourdough Starter** see below)
¾ cup warm water (105-115°)
1 teaspoon active dry yeast
2 teaspoons sugar
1 teaspoon salt
2 ½ cups all-purpose flour, plus extra for flouring
½ cup white chocolate, melted
Olive oil, for greasing

In a medium bowl, combine the sourdough starter, water, yeast, and sugar. Set aside for five minutes.

In a separate bowl, whisk together the flour and salt.

Place the flour mixture in the bowl of a stand mixer. Add the yeast mixture and combine on low speed. Add the white chocolate and beat at medium speed for three minutes or until it forms a firm sticky dough. Turn the dough out onto a floured surface and knead for 4 to 6 minutes, until the dough becomes springy and elasticup Form into a ball and place in a greased bowl. Turn once to grease the top. Cover with plastic wrap and let rise in a warm area until doubled, about 1 ½-2 hours.

Punch down the dough. Turn it out onto a lightly floured surface. Form into a narrow oval loaf and place seam down on a greased baking stone sheet. Cover loosely with plastic wrap. Let rise until doubled and puffy, about 45 minutes to one hour. Using a sharp knife, slash two parallel cuts into the top, diagonal to the shape of the loaf.

Preheat oven to 425°. Bake for 25-30 minutes or until the loaves are well-browned and sound hollow inside. Remove from baking sheet to cool completely on a rack.

Sourdough Starter

2 teaspoons active dry yeast
2 cups warm water (105-115°)
2 cups flour

In a separate bowl, whisk together the flour and salt.

Combine the yeast, water and flour in a large crockery or glass jar (do not use metal). Stir with a wooden spoon and let stand uncovered at 70-80° for 4-7 days or until it emits a sour odor. Stir several times each day.

Pineapple Salsa with Chocolate Tortilla Chips

Makes 6-8 Servings

When it's not sweet, chocolate adds a rich, earthy element to foods, which comes across clearly in the chocolate tortillas that form the scoops for this salsa. If you need to store the tortillas before frying, fold up a piece of paper towel with them in a zipper bag to prevent moisture buildup. If you plan to make a lot of tortillas, invest in a tortilla press, which is basically two metal plates with a clamp, between which you smash down the masa. The cilantro really takes the spotlight in the salsa. Just remember to remove the stems and include only the tender leaves. It's a lot of work, but biting into salsa with stems can be texturally unpleasant.

1 cup pineapple, diced
½ cup red bell pepper, diced
1 ½ cups Roma tomatoes, diced
⅓ cup fresh cilantro, chopped
¼ cup red onion, minced
1 tablespoon fresh jalapeno, diced
¼ cup lime juice
¼ teaspoon black pepper
⅛ teaspoon salt
1 batch Chocolate Tortilla Chips (see page 32)

In a small bowl, mix together the pineapple, tomatoes, peppers, onions, cilantro, lime juice, salt, and pepper.

Refrigerate until serving. Serve with Chocolate Tortilla Chips.

Chocolate Tortilla Chips

**3 cup masa harina
1 cup cocoa powder
1 teaspoon salt
1 cup warm water, plus approximately two cups additional
2 teaspoons honey
vegetable oil, for frying**

Whisk together the masa, cocoa powder, and salt in a large bowl. Add two teaspoons honey and 1 cup warm water and mix with your hands. Add more water a tablespoon at a time until a sticky dough comes together. Knead for a few minutes until the dough becomes springy and elastic (Test by forming a small disk: if it cracks around the edges, add more water.) Form the dough into 1 ½-inch balls.

Heat a dry cast-iron skillet over medium-high heat.

Meanwhile, place a ball of dough between two 6-inch circles of parchment paper and use the bottom of a heavy plate to press the dough out until it forms a ⅛-inch thick circle. Peel off the top layer of parchment paper, but use the bottom to support the dough as you transfer it to the hot skillet. Cook for 1-2 minutes on each side. Place on a clean tea towel and keep covered as you repeat the process with the remaining dough balls. The cocoa will make it difficult to see if the tortillas are starting to burn, so watch them carefully.

Once they are all cooked, add enough oil to a large skillet to make a ½-inch deep layer. Heat on medium-high until a small piece of tortilla dropped in forms bubbles around it. Cut or break the tortillas into pieces. Fry in small batches until crispy and drain on paper towels. Lightly salt to taste.

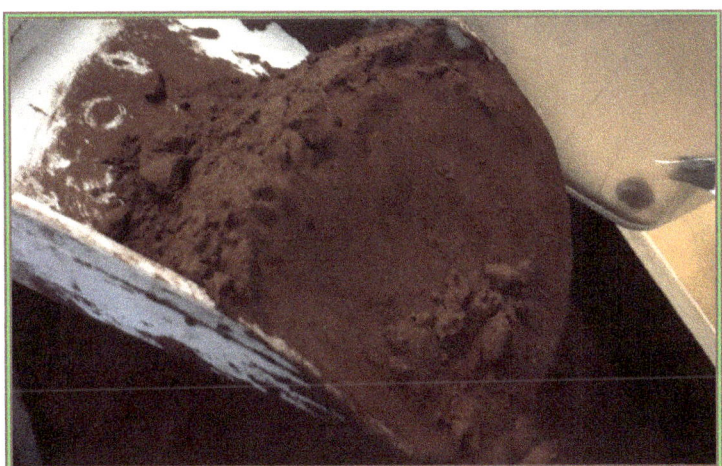

Cheesy Cucumber and Dill Cups

Makes 30 mini-sized cups

There are many ways of using chocolate to add flavors to a dish. Some chocolate-induced flavor notes can be so subtle that they are difficult to identify, but they definitely add a certain complexity. This phyllo dough doesn't scream "chocolate," but it has a particular richness and fragrance from the cocoa butter. When transferring the dough to the tart pan, make sure you press it in well – especially into the corners – so that the dough doesn't puff up excessively while cooking and so flat bases are created for the cups. The dill and cucumber combination results in a fresher-tasting take on a familiar flavor profile.

½ **cup cream cheese, softened**
¼ **cup sour cream**
3 tablespoons fresh dill, chopped
1 ½ tablespoon fresh chives, chopped
2 tablespoons fresh parsley, chopped
1 teaspoon black pepper
¼ **teaspoon salt**
30 Cocoa Butter Phyllo Cups (see page 34)
1 English cucumber, thinly sliced

In a small mixing bowl, combine the cream cheese, sour cream, dill, chives, parsley, salt, and pepper.

Spoon about 1 teaspoon filling into each phyllo shell. Top with a slice of cucumber.

Cocoa Butter Phyllo Cups

**2 cups all-purpose flour, plus more for kneading
5 teaspoons melted cocoa butter
½ teaspoon salt
2 teaspoons rice wine vinegar
¾ cup warm water (105-115°)
½ cup cornstarch
2 tablespoons all-purpose flour**

Preheat oven to 350°.

Place the flour in a large bowl and make a well in the center. Add the cocoa butter, salt, rice wine vinegar, and warm water. Stir until dough just comes together and pulls away from the sides of the bowl, 1-2 minutes. Turn out dough onto lightly floured work surface.

Knead until dough is smooth and elastic. Wrap dough ball in plastic wrap and let rest at room temperature, 1-2 hours.

Divide dough into 20 balls. Cover with plastic wrap to prevent dough from drying out while you work.

Mix the cornstarch and 2 tablespoon flour together in a bowl. Dust a work surface and one of the dough balls with the cornstarch mixture. Roll each ball out into approximately a 5-inch circle. Roll out 4 more dough balls to about the same diameter and stack them on the first one, dusting each layer with more of the cornstarch mixture to keep them from sticking together.

When you have 5 circles, roll again until the 5-layer stack is paper thin, about a 12-inch circle. Place on a sheet of parchment paper and top with another piece of parchment.

Repeat with the remaining balls of dough to create 4 finished sheets of phyllo dough.

Cut out 3-inch circles of dough with either a knife or a cookie/dough cutter. Press each circle into one of the cups of the mini tart pan. Bake 13-15 minutes or until golden brown.

Dark Chocolate Mushroom Arancini

Makes 8-10 Servings

Traditionally, people made arancini to use up leftover risotto. It's amazing how many delicious things result from the need not to waste leftovers. These fried balls, with their gooey, cheesy centers, are no exception. The dark chocolate complements the flavor of the mushrooms in the risotto itself, and the herbs in the panko crust are a nod back to Italy. You can use a commercially prepared Italian herb blend or mix together your own dried herbs. If you blend your own, be sure to include dried oregano, marjoram, thyme, basil, rosemary, and sage.

4 cups **Dark Chocolate Mushroom Risotto,** cooled (see page 37)
1 cup fresh mozzarella, well drained and cubed
½ cup all-purpose flour
½ teaspoon salt
½ teaspoon black pepper
3 eggs, lightly whisked
2 cups panko breadcrumbs
2 tablespoons dried Italian herb blend
2 cups canola oil

Take a spoonful of risotto and fill it with a cube of mozzarella. Shape the risotto into small even balls. Continue the process until all the risotto has been used.

In a small bowl, mix the flour with the salt and pepper. Whisk the eggs in a second bowl. Combine the panko and the Italian seasoning in a third bowl.

Dip each risotto ball into the flour, then into the egg mixture, and then into the breadcrumbs, evenly coating it with each layer. Place on a tray and repeat until all arancini are prepared.

Heat the vegetable oil in a medium saucepan until a dropped in bit of panko sizzles, then fry the arancini in small batches for about 2 minutes or until crispy and golden brown.

Remove from the pan, pat them dry on kitchen paper, and serve immediately.

Dark Chocolate Mushroom Risotto

8 cups chicken broth
3 tablespoons olive oil, divided
1 onion, diced, divided
2 garlic cloves, minced
2 cups fresh baby portobello mushrooms, diced
2 tablespoons fresh thyme, chopped
2 tablespoons fresh Italian parsley, chopped, plus whole sprigs for garnish
2 tablespoons butter
¼ teaspoon salt
¼ teaspoon pepper
2 ounces dark chocolate
1 tablespoon truffle oil
½ ounce dried porcini mushrooms, wiped of grit
2 cups Arborio rice
½ cup dry white wine
½ cup Parmesan cheese, grated

Heat the chicken broth in a medium saucepan and keep warm over low heat. Soak the porcini mushrooms in 1 cup of the chicken stock. Chop finely and set aside.

Heat 2 tablespoons of oil in a Dutch oven over medium heat. Add the onion and garlic and cook, stirring, until translucent, about 5 minutes. Add the fresh mushrooms, herbs, butter, salt, and pepper. Sauté for 3-5 minutes until lightly browned. Drizzle in the truffle oil, then add the reconstituted porcini and the dark chocolate. Sauté until the chocolate melts, then remove from heat and set aside.

Coat a saucepan with the remaining 2 tablespoons of oil. Add the rice and stir quickly until it is well coated and opaque, about 1 minute. Stir in the wine and cook until it is nearly all evaporated.

Add the chicken broth 1 cup at a time, stirring until the rice has absorbed each cup of liquid before adding more. Continue to cook and stir, allowing the rice to absorb each addition of broth before adding more. The risotto should be slightly firm and creamy, not mushy. Add the mushrooms to the rice mixture. Stir in the Parmesan cheese and cook briefly until melted.

Grilled Chicken Satay with White Chocolate Thai-Style Peanut Sauce

Makes 8-10 Servings

Traditionally, Thai peanut sauce is slightly sweet due to the inclusion of sugar. We took that a step further and traded out the sugar for white chocolate, which gives this sauce a richness and velvetiness that pairs well with the chicken. You are likely to wind up with a bit of extra sauce, but it stores well in the refrigerator for future use. Don't skip soaking the skewers when you make the chicken. Even soaked skewers often blacken on the grill, and the soaking keeps them from burning. Lemongrass is one of our favorite herbs, and it gets a chance to shine in this marinade.

5 boneless, skinless chicken thighs
¼ cup lemongrass, roughly chopped
1 shallot, roughly chopped
3 garlic cloves, minced
1 teaspoon cayenne pepper
1 thumb-size piece of ginger, roughly chopped
1 teaspoon dried turmeric
2 tablespoons ground coriander
1 teaspoon cumin
5 tablespoons soy sauce
2 tablespoons fish sauce
6 tablespoons brown sugar
2 tablespoons olive oil
1 batch White Chocolate Thai-Style Peanut Sauce (see page 39)

Cut chicken into strips and place in a gallon-size zipper bag.

In a medium bowl, whisk together the lemongrass, shallot, garlic, cayenne, ginger, turmeric, coriander, cumin, soy sauce, fish sauce, brown sugar, and olive oil. Pour over the chicken and gently squeeze the bag to evenly distribute the marinade. Marinate the meat for two hours or overnight.

When ready to cook, soak the skewers in warm water for an hour before threading on the chicken.

Thread meat onto the skewers, leaving at least the bottom ¼ of the skewer empty.

Thread meat onto the skewers, leaving at least the bottom ¼ of the skewer empty.

Heat a BBQ grill to 300° and place the chicken on the grill in an evenly spaced row. Cook 10-20 minutes or until cooked through, basting occasionally with the leftover marinade.

Serve with White Chocolate Thai-Style Peanut Sauce for dipping.

White Chocolate Thai-Style Peanut Sauce

1 (13.5-ounce) can coconut milk
¼ cup red curry paste
¾ cup natural peanut butter
½ teaspoon salt
¾ cup white chocolate, chopped
2 tablespoons apple cider vinegar

In a medium saucepan, combine the coconut milk, curry paste, peanut butter, salt, white chocolate, and vinegar. Bring to a boil over medium heat, whisking constantly. Simmer the mixture for 3-5 minutes over low heat, continuing to whisk constantly. Remove from heat. Serve immediately or refrigerate.

Sicilian-Style Meatballs with Cocoa Nibs

Makes 10-12 Servings

Sicilian-style meatballs are traditionally made with pine nuts. We've replaced them with cocoa nibs, which lend a similar nutty feel and play well with the sweetness of the currants. They add an interesting texture that doesn't get lost in the intensity of some of the other flavors. These meatballs can stand on their own as an appetizer, but if you have any leftover, they also work well over pasta or as a meatball sandwich filling.

Two (28-ounce) cans crushed peeled Italian tomatoes
¼ cup olive oil
1 teaspoon salt
1 teaspoon black pepper
1 ¼ cup fresh breadcrumbs
4 eggs, beaten
3 garlic cloves, minced
¼ cup flat-leaf parsley, chopped
½ teaspoon dried marjoram
1 teaspoon salt
1 teaspoon black pepper
2 pounds ground beef
½ cup dried currants
¼ cup cocoa nibs
¼ cup Parmesan cheese, freshly grated, plus more for serving
2 cups vegetable oil, for frying

Pour the tomatoes into a large enameled cast-iron casserole and add the olive oil, salt, and pepper. Bring to a boil. Reduce the heat to low and simmer for 30 minutes.

Mash the breadcrumbs together with the eggs. Stir in the garlic, parsley, marjoram, salt, and pepper. Stir until smooth. Add the ground beef, currants, cocoa nibs, and cheese and mix until combined. Form the mixture into 36 (1-inch) meatballs.

Heat the vegetable oil in a large, nonstick skillet. Add the meatballs in 3 batches and fry over moderate heat, turning frequently until browned and cooked through, about 12-13 minutes per batch. Using a slotted spoon, transfer the meatballs to a plate lined with paper towel and allow to drain. Add the meatballs to the sauce and simmer for 30 minutes. Garnish individual servings with additional Parmesan.

Brunch Dishes

In this Chapter you will find:

Basil and Cocoa Breakfast Casserole

Chicken Chilaquiles with Cocoa Red Sauce

Grilled Vegetables with Cocoa Butter Pesto

Cocoa Balsamic Strawberry Spinach Salad

Chocolate Rosemary Pancakes
with Strawberry Balsamic Syrup

Chocolate Chip, Pine Nut,
and Basil Waffles with Orange Syrup

Hazelnut-Filled Tarragon Apple Crepes

Basil and Cocoa Breakfast Casserole

Makes 8 Servings

In this casserole, the cocoa gets pre-cooked with the sausage, giving it a deeper flavor, while the basil gets tossed in with the egg mixture, brightening up the whole dish. And the fresh tomatoes lighten it up a bit. The casserole can be prepared and assembled a day ahead of time and left covered in the refrigerator until you are ready to bake it.

1 (1-pound) tube breakfast sausage
1 cup onion, diced
¼ cup cocoa powder
8 eggs
2 cups milk
½ teaspoon salt
¼ teaspoon black pepper
2 ½ cups potatoes, peeled and shredded
¼ cup basil, chopped
¼ cup spinach, chopped
1 tablespoon fresh sage, minced
2 cups cheddar cheese, shredded
1 cup Roma tomatoes, diced

Preheat the oven to 350°. Butter a 9 x 13-inch baking dish.

In a large skillet, combine the sausage, onion, and baking powder. Cook until the sausage is browned. Set aside.

In a medium bowl, whisk together the eggs, milk, salt, and pepper. Set aside.

To assemble, place half of the shredded potato in the buttered baking dish. Top with half of the sausage mixture, basil, spinach, sage, tomatoes, and cheese. Add the other half of the shredded potatoes, and repeat layering the sausage mixture, basil, spinach, sage, tomatoes, and cheese.

Pour the egg mixture evenly over the casserole. Cover the baking dish with aluminum foil and bake for 1 hour. Uncover and bake for an additional 15 minutes. Let stand for 10 minutes and serve.

Chicken Chilaquiles with Cocoa Red Sauce

Makes 4 Servings

Every time we've had chilaquiles, it's either been for breakfast or as a late-night snack. There are a ton of interpretations of this dish – which can be done with either red or green sauce. It can be served with re-fried beans or sliced avocado. You'll notice that most of these ingredients (such as shredded chicken and stale tortillas) could be leftovers. If you don't have any leftover chicken to shred, you can top each serving with one or two fried eggs instead.

12 stale corn tortillas (leave out overnight)
4 Roma tomatoes, cut in half
4 dried arbol chilies, stems and seeds removed
1-6 dried puya chilies, stems and seeds removed
3 tablespoons canola oil, plus more for frying
3-4 garlic cloves, peeled and halved
1 teaspoon tomato-chicken bullion powder
3 ounces dark chocolate, melted
1 teaspoon salt
4 sprigs of cilantro, stems removed, chopped
1 epazote leaf
1 ½ cup chicken breast, cooked and shredded
1 ounce queso Cotija or 4 ounces queso fresco or queso Chihuahua, crumbled
½ cup white onion, cut into rings
Mexican crema

Stack the tortillas and cut them into 6 even triangles.

Bring about 3 cups of water to boil in a small pot and then turn down to a simmer.

Meanwhile, in a medium skillet over medium heat, heat 2 tablespoons of canola oil. Very quickly fry the arbol and puya chilies in the oil, turning constantly until they darken – but do not allow them to blacken. Once the chilies are fried, add them to the simmering water.

Add the garlic cloves to the pan and fry until golden. Place them in the pot of simmering water. Next, fry the tomatoes until they soften, and then add them to the simmering water. Remove the softened vegetables from the water with a slotted spoon, draining well, and transfer them to a blender. Discard water.

In the blender, add the bullion powder, salt, cilantro, epazote, and melted chocolate to the vegetable mixture. Blend until smooth.

Add the shredded chicken and mix with a spoon into the sauce. Set aside.

Add enough oil to fully cover the bottom of the skillet to a ½-inch depth and heat until a bit of tortilla dropped into it sizzles. Fry the tortilla pieces in several batches until they are crisp and golden brown. Avoid overcrowding the skillet, and flip them over only once. Drain on a plate lined with paper towels.

Once all of the tortillas are fried, drain all but a teaspoon of the oil from the pan. Return the frying pan to the heat and add all of the tortilla chips. Once you hear them start to pop, add the salsa to the pan and coat the chips well.

Add the cheese and cover for a few minutes to melt, but do not let the chips become too soggy. Serve the chilaquiles on 4 plates and garnish with cilantro, cheese, and onions. Drizzle a small amount of Mexican crema on top.

Grilled Vegetables with Cocoa Butter Pesto

Makes 8 Servings

Cocoa butter solidifies easily, so if you prepare the pesto for this dish ahead of time, make sure it is in a microwave-safe container so that you can reliquefy the pesto before pouring it over the vegetables. Pesto is traditionally made with olive oil. Whether you use the cocoa butter (which gives this pesto a delicate fragrance) or go for the more traditional olive oil, making pesto is a great way to preserve the bounty of the summer herb garden. You can scale this pesto recipe up and spoon the extra into an ice cube tray. Once frozen, the pesto cubes can be popped out and stored in a zipper bag in the freezer for other uses. We like the contrast in color and texture in the vegetables we've chosen for this dish, but you can add your favorite veggies to the mix.

1 sweet potato, peeled and cut lengthwise into ½-inch thick slices
1 large eggplant, trimmed and cut lengthwise into ½-inch thick slices
2 zucchinis, trimmed and cut lengthwise into ½-inch thick slices
2 yellow squash, trimmed and cut lengthwise into ½-inch thick slices
2 ears of corn, shucked
2 red bell peppers, seeded and cut lengthwise into quarters
olive oil, for brushing
salt, to taste
black pepper, to taste
1 batch Cocoa Butter Pesto (see page 145)

Heat a grill to 400° and oil the grill rack.

Brush the sweet potato, eggplant, zucchini, squash, and corn with olive oil. Season the vegetables on both sides with salt and pepper.

Place the bell peppers skin side down on the grill. Place the eggplant, zucchini, squash, and corn on the grill. Roast the peppers until the skins are blistered and charred. Roast the corn, turning until cooked evenly and softened. Roast the eggplant, zucchini, and squash until lightly charred and softened.

Cut the corn kernels from the cobs and place in a large bowl. Cut the sweet potato, eggplant, zucchini, and squash into ½-inch diced pieces and add to the bowl. Peel the charred skin away from the bell peppers, cut the peppers into ½-inch pieces and add to the bowl. Add the cocoa butter pesto and toss gently to coat the vegetables. Season with salt and pepper. Serve immediately.

Cocoa Balsamic Strawberry Spinach Salad

Makes 6 Servings

While the same chocolate balsamic in the marinated strawberries is also used in the salad dressing for this dish, the sugar added with the strawberries highlights the sweetness and caramel flavor – while in the salad dressing, the honey mustard and garlic transform it into something more savory. Yet the two elements work well together. Any leftover salad dressing will keep well in the refrigerator for several weeks.

1 pound boneless, skinless chicken breast
1 tablespoon olive oil
2 (5-ounce) bags pre-washed spinach
½ cup Chocolate Balsamic Vinaigrette (see page 146)
¼ cup Parmesan cheese, finely shredded
¼ cup pecans, chopped
½ cup Chocolate Balsamic Strawberries, drained (see page 146)

In a medium skillet, sauté the chicken in olive oil. Dice. Set aside. Place the spinach in a large bowl and add the vinaigrette, Parmesan cheese, pecans, strawberries and chicken. Toss salad together and serve immediately.

Cocoa Honey Fruit Salad

Makes 8 Servings

Honey is such a versatile ingredient. It is usually classified by the flower-source the bees took the nectar from to make the honey. (Some, such as buckwheat honey, can be quite strong.) This recipe uses a more subtle wildflower honey with the cocoa powder blended right into it. You can also use cocoa-infused honey on bread or waffles or to sweeten beverages. If you'd prefer to omit the alcohol here, just use orange juice in place of the banana liqueur.

**½ cup wildflower honey
2 tablespoons banana liqueur
2 tablespoons cocoa powder
2 cups clementine segments
2 cups papaya, peeled and diced
2 cup blackberries
2 cup pineapple, peeled and diced
1 ½ cups flaked coconut, plus extra to garnish
½ cup pecans
1 tablespoon fresh mint
1 tablespoon fresh basil**

Whisk together the honey, orange juice, and cocoa powder.

Place the clementine segments, papaya, blackberries, pineapple, pecans, and coconut in a large bowl. Pour honey mixture over fruit and toss to coat. Add the mint and basil and refrigerate for at least two hours. Garnish with additional coconut just before serving.

Chocolate Rosemary Pancakes with Strawberry Balsamic Syrup

Makes Around 10 (6-inch) Pancakes

When you're a kid, chocolate chip pancakes are a rare opportunity to basically have dessert for breakfast. This recipe is a riff on that remembered flavor from childhood – with a little sophistication. This cocoa-powder based pancake isn't as sweet as the chocolate chip variety, and it has a few savory elements in the form of black pepper, balsamic vinegar, and rosemary. Plus, you are pairing chocolate and strawberries, which many equate with elegance or romance. Rosemary has such a unique resinous flavor; it is a joy to cook with. In addition, it is an easy herb to grow, complete with such beautiful flowers. The name "rosemary" actually comes from Latin words meaning "dew" and "sea" or roughly translated "dew of the sea," because in some areas, no additional water past the morning dew is required to make it grow.

1 ½ cup flour
⅓ cup cocoa powder
3 tablespoons sugar
1 teaspoon baking powder
½ teaspoon baking soda
1 teaspoon salt
1 ½ cups milk
1 tablespoon lemon juice
3 tablespoon butter, melted
2 eggs
1 teaspoon rosemary needles, finely minced
½ teaspoon vanilla
Butter, for serving
1 batch **Strawberry Balsamic Syrup** (see page 147)

Whisk the flour, cocoa powder, sugar, baking powder, baking soda, and salt together in a large bowl.

In a medium bowl, combine the milk and lemon juice. Let the milk mixture sit for a minute to curdle, then add the melted butter and stir. Add the eggs, rosemary, and vanilla and stir until well combined.

Pour the milk mixture into the flour mixture. Mix until the dry ingredients are just incorporated (don't worry about any small lumps).

Heat a large nonstick skillet or griddle. Pour a ladleful of the batter onto the griddle. Flip the pancake when all the bubbles have popped and cook the batter through. Repeat with the remaining batter.

Serve hot with butter and Strawberry Balsamic Syrup.

Chocolate Chip, Pine Nut, and Basil Waffles with Orange Syrup

Makes Around 6 (7-inch) Waffles

These waffles, with their combination of pine nuts and basil leaves, echo the classic flavors of pesto – with a sweet and chocolatey twist. The basil also combines with the orange in the syrup, completely transforming the fruit's sweetness into something special. Oranges are grown throughout the southern peninsula of Italy, whereas pesto originated in the northern part of the country. The word "pesto" means "to pound," referring to the way the leaves were originally broken down. But for the purposes of this recipe, it is easier to stack all of the basil leaves on top of each other, roll them into a tube, and snip them into thin shards using a pair of sharp scissors. Roughly chopping the pine nuts instead of grinding them gives the finished waffle a bit of crunch. The nuts of all varieties of pine are edible, but only about 20 species of pine trees produce nuts large enough to be worth the time it takes to harvest them.

1 ¾ cup cake flour, sifted before measuring
2 teaspoon baking powder
½ teaspoon salt
1 tablespoon sugar
3 egg yolks
2-7 tablespoons melted butter
1 ½ cups milk
½ cup pine nuts, chopped
1 cup bittersweet chocolate, chopped
6-8 basil leaves
Butter, for serving
1 batch **Basil Orange Syrup**, for serving (see page 147)

Resift the flour with the baking powder, salt, and sugar.

In a separate bowl, beat the egg yolks. Add the melted butter and milk. Pour the milk mixture into the flour mixture and stir until well combined. Stir in the pine nuts and chocolate.

Heat a waffle iron and cook the batter according to the manufacturer's directions.

Hazelnut-Filled Tarragon Apple Crepes

Makes Around 8 (5-inch) Crepes

In France, a popular take-out treat is a hazelnut-chocolate-filled crepe. There's just something about the crispness of a freshly made crepe that perfectly accents the creaminess of the hazelnut-chocolate spread. Just remember that if you go too heavy applying the hazelnut-chocolate spread, you won't be able to taste all the flavors in the crepe. We added tarragon (one of the four fines herbs of French cooking) and apple butter (apples are a staple in Normandy) to the crepe batter. We used dried tarragon here because we find it slightly sweeter than the fresh. Any extra crepes are flavorful enough to serve on their own or could be filled with ham and cheese.

¾ cup all-purpose flour, sifted after measuring
½ teaspoon salt
1 teaspoon double-acting baking powder
2 tablespoons powdered sugar
1 egg
¼ cup apple butter
1 cup milk
⅔ cup water
1 tablespoon dried tarragon
1 teaspoon lemon zest
oil, for greasing
hazelnut-chocolate spread
powdered sugar, for garnish
cocoa powder, for garnish

Resift the flour into a large bowl together with the salt, baking powder, and sugar.

In a separate medium bowl, beat the egg lightly. Add the milk, water, lemon zest, and tarragon. Pour the egg mixture into the flour mixture. Stir the ingredients until just incorporated, ignoring any lumps. Let the batter rest in the refrigerator for an hour before cooking.

Place a 5-inch skillet over medium heat, and grease it with a few drops of oil. Pour in a small amount of batter. Tip the skillet until the batter has spread over the bottom. Cook the pancake over moderate heat, flipping it when the batter loses its gloss. Repeat with the remaining batter, making sure to add additional oil between each pancake.

Spread one half of each crepe with the hazelnut-chocolate spread, leaving a ½-inch edge and fold it in half and then in half again. Place two on a plate and sprinkle with powdered sugar and cocoa powder. Serve immediately.

Entrees

In this Chapter you will find:

Fruit and Cocoa-Stuffed Pork Loin

Cocoa-Rubbed Skirt Steak with Gremolata

Chocolate BBQ Ribs

Black Mole Chicken

Cocoa Honey Fruit Salad

Chocolate Chili

Chocolate Coq au Vin

Lentil Stew
with Sour Cream Drizzle

Herbed Pumpkin Ravioli
with Cocoa Brown Butter Sauce

Cheesy Pear and Chocolate Tortellini

Cocoa and Herb Fettuccine with Garlic Alfredo

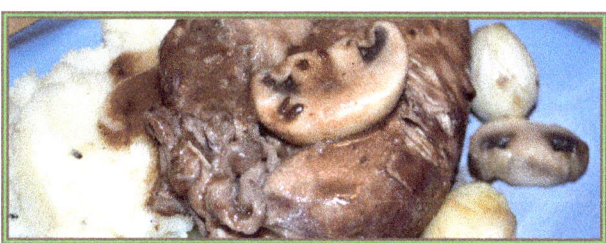

Fruit and Cocoa-Stuffed Pork Loin

Makes Around 8 Servings

The word "sage" comes from the Latin word "salvere," which means "to save." We're not sure whether that has to do with the fact that it was sometimes used as an aid in food preservation (it functions as a food antioxidant) or if it comes from the antimicrobial properties that made it an essential medicinal herb (it's probably the second one – sage was included in the "thieves' herbs," thought to protect against even the most contagious illness). Here it merely adds a peppery note to the fruit mixture that fills the pork loin. Make sure that you have some sort of liquid in the roasting pan, even if it doesn't reach the height of the rack the pork is on. Otherwise, the juices from the pork will burn on the bottom of the pan.

1 (4-pound) boneless pork loin
1 ½ teaspoon salt, divided
1 ½ teaspoon black pepper, divided
3 cups diced dried fruit
¼ cup cocoa nibs
2 tablespoons dark brown sugar
1 tablespoon fresh sage, chopped
¼ teaspoon dried crushed red pepper
1 cup dry white wine
2 tablespoons olive oil
5 cups water

Bring the dried fruit, cocoa nibs, brown sugar, sage, red pepper, and white wine to a boil in a small saucepan over medium-high heat. Cook 2 minutes, stirring occasionally. Remove from heat and cool completely (about 40 minutes).

Meanwhile, butterfly the pork loin by making a lengthwise cut down the center of one flat side, cutting to within ½-inch of other side. (Do not cut all the way through the pork.) Open the pork, forming a rectangle, and place between two sheets of heavy-duty plastic wrap. Flatten to ½-inch thickness using a meat mallet or rolling pin. Sprinkle with ½ teaspoon each salt and pepper.

Spoon the fruit mixture over the pork, leaving a ½-inch border around edges. Roll up the pork, jelly-roll fashion, starting at one long side. Tie with kitchen string at 1 ½-inch intervals. Sprinkle with the remaining 1 teaspoon salt and 1 teaspoon pepper.

Preheat oven to 375°.

Meanwhile, over medium-high heat in a large pan, brown the pork in hot oil on all sides (about 2-3 minutes per side). Place seam side down on broiling rack in a roasting pan. Add 5 cups of water and any remaining fruit.

Bake for 1 hour or until a meat thermometer inserted into the thickest portion of the stuffing registers 135°. Cover loosely with aluminum foil and let stand 15 minutes before serving.

Cocoa-Rubbed Skirt Steak with Gremolata

Makes Around 8 Servings

Gremolata comes from Italy, but the cocoa-spice rub we concocted for the meat had more of a Southwestern feel to it, so we decided to put it on skirt steak. In addition to giving a huge punch of flavor, the gremolata adds a nicely contrasting color to this dish. Don't overcook the steak, as this cut of meat can get tough.

2 tablespoons olive oil
1 tablespoon dried oregano
2 teaspoons dried basil
2 teaspoons paprika
¼ teaspoon crushed red pepper flakes
1 tablespoon cocoa powder
1 teaspoon salt
1 teaspoon black pepper
3 garlic cloves, minced
2 pounds skirt steak
1 batch **Gremolata** (see page 60)

In a small bowl, combine the olive oil, oregano, basil, paprika, red pepper flakes, cocoa powder, salt, pepper, and garlic. Rub the mixture onto the steak. Wrap with plastic wrap and marinate for 1 hour or overnight.

When ready to cook, heat a grill to 300° and place the steak on the grill. Grill meat to desired doneness, then serve topped with gremolata.

Gremolata

2 teaspoons lemon zest
4 garlic cloves, minced
¼ cup flat-leaf parsley, hard packed, minced

Combine the lemon zest, garlic, and parsley in a small bowl. Refrigerate for at least two hours to allow the flavors to mingle.

Chocolate BBQ Ribs

Makes 4 Servings

BBQ sauce started out as a way to preserve meat in the era before refrigeration. It was a crude substance, mainly salt or vinegar. But as cooks discovered how much a specific blend of ingredients could change the character of meat, they turned BBQ sauce into an art form. In the United States alone, there are at least 7 regional BBQ traditions (not to mention the innumerable variations found in global kitchens) that celebrate the way herbs and spices can improve the flavor of meat. It was only a matter of time before someone added chocolate to the mix.

Never use aluminum when working with vinegar – choose stainless steel and glass containers and wooden spoons.

4 pounds beef ribs
¼ cup garlic powder
¼ cup onion powder
¼ cup salt
1 batch Chocolate BBQ Sauce (see page 62)

Preheat oven to 250°.

Rinse and dry the ribs with a paper towel.

Combine the garlic powder, onion powder and salt. Rub the ribs with the mixture, making sure to coat the ribs evenly.

Place on a baking sheet with a lip and cook in the oven for 2 hours. At an hour and a half, heat a grill to 350°. After 2 hours, remove the ribs from the oven and place on the grill to finish cooking. Baste with the chocolate BBQ sauce during grilling. Cook until the BBQ sauce thickens on the outside of the ribs, turning as needed.

Chocolate BBQ Sauce

**5 cups tomatoes, cored and chopped
½ cup onions, minced
2 garlic cloves, minced
1 sprig cilantro, stem removed
½ tablespoon dried red pepper flakes
1 ½ tablespoons chipotle chili powder
¾ teaspoon celery seeds
¼ cup dark brown sugar, packed
¼ cup apple cider vinegar
1 ½ tablespoons lemon juice
1 ½ teaspoons salt
1 tablespoon black pepper
1 teaspoon dry mustard
¼ teaspoon ground ginger
½ teaspoon ground cumin
¾ teaspoon paprika
½ teaspoon ground cinnamon
¾ cup cocoa powder**

In a large pot over high heat, combine the tomatoes, onions, garlic, hot pepper flakes, chipotle chili powder, and celery seeds. Bring the mixture to a boil, stirring constantly, then reduce heat to medium-low. Cover the pot and simmer for 30 minutes, stirring occasionally. Remove the pot from the heat, and allow the mixture to cool partially. Process this mixture through a food mill (discarding solids) into a large bowl. In a large pot over medium-high heat, combine the tomato mixture with the brown sugar, apple cider vinegar, lemon juice, salt, black pepper, mustard, ginger, cumin, paprika, cinnamon, and cocoa powder. Bring the mixture to a boil, then reduce the heat to medium-low and simmer, stirring frequently, for 30 minutes or until the sauce has thickened to the desired consistency.

Herbie Info Box

Cilantro is one of those foods that individuals either love or hate. (There are several websites dedicated to the abhorrence of cilantro, and some people are even trying to ban its use in restaurants.) If cilantro does not appeal to you, by all means omit it. A recent study proposes that your like or dislike of cilantro may be based on one specific gene in the cluster of genes that govern a person's sense of smell. The gene (OR6A2) is extremely sensitive to the aldehyde chemicals that give cilantro its distinctive flavor. A person may have one copy of this gene or two – and if you have two, you are statistically more inclined to think cilantro tastes like soap. However, not all study participants who have duplicates of this gene reported dislike of the herb, which suggests that other factors may be involved in the perception of cilantro. But the point we take away from this is that a food's scent influences how its flavor is perceived. When we are putting together a combination of herbs (especially if it is going into a dish with raw eggs or other ingredients that make it inadvisable to taste until the cooking is done), we like to take samples of each of the herbs we intend to use and rub them together. The fragrance will usually tell us if we are going to like the finished dish.

Black Mole Chicken

Makes Around 4 Servings

Mole is one of those dishes that has as many variations as there are cooks who make it. Three Mexican states claim to have invented it (Pueblo, Tlaxcala, and Oaxaca), and there are numerous legends surrounding its origin (the most famous involving impoverished nuns cooking up all the odds and ends in the convent kitchen to impress a visiting dignitary). One thing is certain: mole, which combines ingredients native to Europe, North America, and Africa, was the first truly international dish created in the Americas. Many people associate mole only with mole poblano. However, the word simply means "sauce," and is used to indicate mixtures both with and without chocolate, some of which may be red or green instead of dark. The main ingredient all mole sauces share is chilies. One of the darkest, richest moles is Oaxacan Black Mole, which includes a number of fresh and dried herbs.

If you find a turkey on sale, feel free to use it in this recipe in place of the chicken, as turkey with mole sauce is actually more traditional. This recipe can be overpoweringly fragrant due to released plant oils that can irritate your eyes or make you cough, especially when you are roasting the chilies, so ventilate your kitchen well.

1 tomato, diced
2 slices of French or Italian bread
1 large chicken, cut into 8 pieces
8 garlic cloves, peeled, plus 6 cloves
2 onions, sliced and divided
4 sprigs peppermint
1 teaspoon salt
2 ounces cascabel chilies, dried, stems removed
½ ounce pasillas chilies, dried, stems removed
1 ½ ounces mulatos chilies, dried, stems removed
½ cup water
2 cloves
2 allspice berries
1 (1 ½-inch) cinnamon stick, roughly crushed
½ teaspoon marjoram, dried
1 teaspoon fresh thyme leaves, minced
1 tablespoon fresh Mexican oregano leaves, minced, plus extra for garnish
¼ cup vegetable shortening
2 tablespoons sesame seeds, plus extra for garnish
2 tablespoons peanuts
2 tablespoons slivered almonds
2 tablespoons raisins
1 small ripe plantain, peeled and sliced
1 corn tortilla, torn into pieces
¼ cup vegetable oil
1 ounce bittersweet chocolate, coarsely chopped
3 cups cooked white rice, for serving

Preheat the oven to 450°.
Spread the diced tomatoes on a baking sheet and roast them in the preheated oven for 10-20 minutes or until the edges begin to char. Set aside to cool.

Remove the seeds (reserving them) from all the chiles. Spread the dried chilies on a baking sheet. Toast the chilies for 5 minutes or until almost charred. Place the chilies in a bowl and rinse with cold water. Drain off the cold water. Add enough hot water to cover the chilies, and set aside to soak for half an hour.

Reduce oven temperature to 300. Place the slices of bread on a baking sheet and place in oven for 8 minutes or until completely dried out. Set aside.

Combine the cloves, allspice, marjoram, and cinnamon stick in a spice grinder and process until you have a uniform powder. Set aside.

In a large pot, combine the chicken, garlic, mint, and onions and add enough water to cover over. Bring to a boil over high heat, then reduce the heat to medium and simmer the chicken until it is cooked through and tender (around 30-40 minutes). Remove the chicken from the cooking liquid. Set aside. Strain the broth through a piece of cheesecloth into a clean bowl. Measure out 2 cups of broth (reserving the rest for another use). Set the broth aside.

Meanwhile, place the reserved chili seeds into an ungreased skillet over medium-high heat. Shaking the pan or stirring frequently, toast the seeds until they are fragrant and blackened. Transfer to a medium bowl and cover with cold water. Set aside to soak for about 10 minutes. Drain (discarding the liquid) and place the seeds into a blender. Add the ½ cup water, tomatoes, thyme, oregano, and spice mixture. Leave this mixture in the blender.

Heat the vegetable shortening in a medium skillet over medium heat. Add the sesame seeds, peanuts, almonds, and raisins. Fry for about 10-20 seconds or until the nuts turn golden. Skim the raisins, nuts, and seeds out of the hot shortening. Transfer this mixture to the blender and pulse with the tomato mixture until smooth. Repeat frying and pulsing with the garlic cloves, onion, plantain, tortilla, and dried bread. Add additional water if needed to keep the blender blades working.

Heat the vegetable oil in a large pot over medium-low heat. Pour in the tomato mixture and stir-fry for 12-15 minutes, stirring frequently. Meanwhile, put 2 cups of the chili soaking water in the blender. Add 3-4 of the chilies and blend until smooth. Repeat with the remaining chilies. Add the chilies to the tomato mixture and stir to combine. Add the chocolate. Cook for 4-6 minutes.

Add 2 cups of the chicken broth and continue cooking, stirring occasionally and adding more broth if necessary, for 30-40 minutes or until thick enough to coat the back of a spoon. Add the chicken and cook for 10-12 minutes. Add additional salt if needed.

Serve over cooked rice, garnished with a sprinkling of minced oregano and sesame seeds.

Herbie Info Box

This recipe calls for Mexican oregano. Oregano is one of those common plant names which can describe a few different plants that taste similar but that are not the same species. Most recipes that call for "oregano" are referring to the mild, Mediterranean relative of the mint family, which can be sweeter and more peppery than the other similarly named herbs. Mexican oregano (a member of the Vervain family) is more closely related to lemon verbena, which gives it some citrus notes and also a mild anise flavor. In a pinch, you can substitute regular oregano for Mexican oregano. Oregano is sometimes called "wild marjoram." This is because it is much more closely related to marjoram than it is to Mexican oregano.

Chocolate Chili

Makes Around 4 Servings

Chili is one of those recipes that can spark contention. Some people only do vegetarian chilies, while others believe that chili really isn't chili of there are beans in it. (This recipe is adaptable. If you prefer all meat or all beans, just substitute an extra pound of ground beef or an extra couple cups of kidney beans to keep the volume roughly the same.)

Different cooks also look to a variety of "secret" ingredients to add thickness and depth of flavor to their chili. For instance, the 2012 winner of the Annual World's Championship Chili Cookoff (as regulated by the International Chili Society) included prunes. We, however, prefer to get our chili's hit of fruity sweetness from good quality bittersweet chocolate. We also like adding a good dose of cilantro to round out the flavor. Many sources consider adding chocolate to chili a nod to Mexican mole, but chili is not Mexican in origin (although there is a definite Spanish influence). Chili's southwestern roots are probably based in Texas, where trail cooks heading for California concocted stackable blocks of fat and chili peppers, which could be rehydrated as needed.

2 tablespoons olive oil
½ cup onion, chopped, plus extra for garnish
2 garlic cloves, pressed
1 pound ground beef
1 cup tomatoes, diced
2 cups kidney beans, cooked
1 teaspoon salt
1 teaspoon black pepper
1 bay leaf
2 tablespoons chili powder
1 ½ ounces bittersweet chocolate
½ cup red wine
1 tablespoon chipotle in adobo
1 tablespoon minced cilantro
Cornbread or cooked rice, for serving
Cheddar cheese, shredded, for garnish

Heat the olive oil in the bottom of a large pot. Add the onion and garlic and cook, stirring frequently, until the onion becomes translucent. Add the ground beef and brown through. Drain off any excess fat. Stir in the tomatoes, beans, salt, pepper, bay leaf, chili powder, chocolate, water, and chipotle. Simmer covered for an hour or longer, stirring occasionally. Remove the bay leaf. Stir in the cilantro.

Serve with cornbread or over rice. Garnish each serving with onion and cheese.

Chocolate Coq au Vin
Makes Around 4 Servings

Coq au vin roughly translates from the French as "old rooster in wine sauce." It is one of those dishes that started out as a way to make what was on hand more palatable but turned out to be incredibly delicious (Julia Child made this particular dish popular and often demonstrated it on her cooking shows). While braising would certainly benefit a tough bird, it makes an average chicken incredibly tender. While coq au vin is traditionally served with egg noodles, we prefer mashed potatoes, because the potatoes soak up the delectable sauce. The sauce can be thickened with a roux added at the beginning of cooking, but many French country cooks thicken the sauce with chocolate added just at the end of cooking time. The herbs used in this dish (thyme, parsley and bay) are those that usually make up a bouquet garni (a method for adding herbs that are to be removed at the end of the cooking time that involves bundling a bouquet of herbs with string or in cheesecloth) although that step is not necessary here, as the sauce will be strained.

3 cups Burgundy wine
1 onion, sliced
1 carrot, sliced
4 garlic cloves, pressed
2 sprigs parsley, plus extra for garnish
2 sprigs thyme
1 bay leaf
1 large chicken, cut into 8 pieces
1 teaspoon salt
¼ cup flour
¼ cup olive oil
8 ounces white mushrooms, sliced
¼ cup apple brandy
1 ½ cups chicken stock
2 cups pearl onions, peeled
1 ounce unsweetened chocolate, chopped
black pepper, to taste
4 cups mashed potatoes, for serving

In a medium saucepan over medium heat, combine the Burgundy, onion, carrot, garlic, parsley, thyme, and bay leaf. Bring this mixture to a simmer and cook for approximately 5 minutes. Remove the saucepan from the heat and allow the mixture to cool completely. Place the chicken pieces in a large zipper bag and pour the cooled marinade over them. Place the bag in a large bowl and refrigerate overnight.
The next day, remove the chicken pieces from the marinade and pat each one dry. Strain the marinade liquid into a medium saucepan (reserving solids). Place the saucepan over low heat and bring the liquid to a simmer. Cook for 5 minutes, then strain to remove any foam that has formed.

Dredge each of the chicken pieces in the flour and then sprinkle with salt. Heat a couple of tablespoons of the oil in a Dutch oven over high heat and add two or three of the chicken pieces and brown on all sides. Place the browned chicken on a platter and repeat with the remaining chicken, adding additional oil if necessary. Add the vegetables and the reserved mushroom stems to the Dutch oven. Brown the vegetables, then remove them to the serving platter.

Deglaze the Dutch oven with the apple brandy, making sure to scrape up any browned bits. Add the chicken stock, marinade, chicken pieces, and browned vegetables. Stir to combine. Cover the Dutch oven and simmer the mixture until the chicken is completely cooked through (around 2 hours).

Meanwhile, heat the remaining oil in a large skillet over medium heat. Add the pearl onions and cook, stirring frequently, until softened all the way through and browned on the outside. Remove the onions from the skillet and place them in a large bowl. Place the mushrooms in the skillet and cook, stirring frequently, until browned. Add them to the large bowl alongside the onions. Use tongs to remove the cooked chicken pieces from the liquid and place in the bowl with the onions and mushrooms.

Strain the cooking liquid into a separate large bowl (discarding solids). Skim the fat from the surface of this liquid. Return the liquid to the Dutch oven and simmer until slightly reduced. Place the chocolate in a small bowl and add ½ cup of the cooking liquid. Stir until the chocolate is smooth, then add the chocolate mixture to the cooking liquid. Stir to incorporate. Add the chicken, onions, and mushrooms to the Dutch oven and heat everything through. Place a large dollop of mashed potatoes on a plate, add one or two pieces of the chicken, and spoon the sauce, onions, and mushrooms over it. Garnish with chopped parsley and serve immediately.

Lentil Stew with Cilantro Sour Cream Drizzle

Makes Around 8 Servings

Lentils have such a mild flavor, they make a versatile canvas for other flavors. The ancho pepper powder and the dark chocolate make for a rich base. Keep an eye on the lentils, especially during the final stage of cooking. They may need additional liquid, as dried lentils will vary as to how much liquid they can absorb. If you want a thicker sauce, reduce the amount of lime juice.

7 cups chicken stock
½ cup onion, diced
2 celery stalks, finely diced
1 carrot, peeled and finely diced
2 cups dry lentils
1 teaspoon ground cumin
1 teaspoon ground ancho chilies
1 teaspoon salt
1 teaspoon black pepper
2 ounces dark chocolate
1 batch Cilantro Sour Cream Drizzle, for serving (see below)

Bring 1 cup stock to a boil in a large pot. Add the onion, celery and carrot and cook, uncovered, stirring frequently for 7-8 minutes. Add the lentils, cumin, ancho chili, salt, black pepper, and remaining stock. Season with salt to taste. Bring to a boil and immediately reduce heat to a simmer. Cook uncovered until the lentils have softened and are cooked through, 35-40 minutes. Add the unsweetened chocolate and stir until completely melted.

When the lentils are soft, ladle soup into bowls and drizzle the Cilantro Sour Cream Drizzle over them. Serve immediately.

Cilantro Sour Cream Drizzle

½ cup sour cream
½ cup cilantro, stems removed, minced
¾ cup lime juice
½ teaspoon salt
¼ teaspoon black pepper

In a blender, combine the sour cream, cilantro, lime juice, salt, and pepper. Blend until it forms a smooth, liquid sauce. Refrigerate until needed.

Herbed Pumpkin Ravioli with Cocoa Brown Butter Sauce

Makes 6-8 Servings

This pumpkin ravioli is completely savory, with the cocoa brown butter making a nutty counterpoint to the luxurious pumpkin. If you plan on making ravioli often, invest in either a square or round ravioli cutter so that you can get a consistent size and shape, along with a pretty edge. It's more traditional to do pumpkin-chocolate ravioli in sage butter sauce, but we wanted to flip things around and put the herbs in the pumpkin filling and the chocolate in the sauce. Dark chocolate can also be grated over this (or your favorite) pasta dish as a garnish.

4 eggs
2 ⅔ cups semolina flour
1 cup pumpkin puree
½ cup Parmesan cheese, grated, plus extra for topping
1 egg yolk
2 teaspoons rubbed sage
2 teaspoons dried oregano
1 teaspoon salt
½ teaspoon black pepper
¼ cup butter
1 tablespoon cocoa powder

Place the semolina flour in a medium bowl. Make a well and add two of the whole eggs. Stir to combine and form a sticky dough. Pour out onto a floured surface and knead until the dough is no longer sticky and has become elastic. Divide the dough into two portions, wrap in plastic wrap, and set aside for at least an hour.

In a medium bowl, combine the pumpkin puree, Parmesan cheese, egg yolk, sage, oregano, salt, and pepper. Set aside.

When ready to continue, fill a large pot two-thirds full with water and set to boil over medium-high heat.

Meanwhile, roll out one half of the pasta dough into a long thin rectangle. Along one long side of the rectangle, place one-tablespoon scoops of the filling two inches apart. Wet the dough with water around each scoop of filling. Fold the opposite side of the rectangular dough over the scoops, pressing down firmly at the edges to remove excess air inside the pockets. Cut the filled pockets into squares or rounds, ensuring each ravioli is sealed thoroughly. Add a drop of additional water between any layers that are not sticking and press down again. Repeat with the second half of the pasta dough. Re-roll the dough scraps and form additional ravioli as necessary. (You may not need all the dough if you roll it thinly enough.)

In small batches, add the ravioli to the boiling water. Boil for 3 minutes, flip over and boil for another 3 minutes. Drain the ravioli in a colander.

Meanwhile, heat a skillet over medium-low heat and add the butter. Stir the butter frequently, skimming off any foam that forms on the surface. Cook until the butter turns golden brown. Add the cocoa powder and stir until combined. Add the boiled ravioli and cook for 4 to 5 additional minutes, flipping the ravioli several times. Serve hot, spooning any leftover sauce over the ravioli. Garnish with additional grated Parmesan cheese.

Cheesy Pear and Chocolate Tortellini

Makes Around 4 Servings

This tortellini walks that sweet-savory edge, with complex flavors that blend delicately. The lemon-wine sauce gives each bite a bit of a citrusy edge that gives way to the more subtle filling elements. Asian pears are one of our favorite fruits, because they have a refreshing floral taste. Parsley is also an especially refreshing herb, so we added that to the pasta dough. We also have an affinity for parsley, because it is one of the plants that attracts black swallowtail butterflies to the herb garden. We've planted extra just for them!

7 ounces orange chocolate Wensleydale cheese (or regular Wensleydale plus additional chocolate chips), crumbled
½ cup mascarpone cheese
2 Asian pears, peeled, cored, grated and dried off by pressing with paper towels
¼ cup mini chocolate chips
2 ⅔ cups flour, plus more for flouring
4 eggs
3 tablespoons fresh parsley, minced
1 tablespoon fresh basil, minced
2 large lemons, zested and juiced
½ cup olive oil
½ cup dry white wine
¼ teaspoon black pepper

In a large bowl, combine the Wensleydale, mascarpone, pears, and chocolate chips. Chill until ready to use.

Mix the flour and eggs until a sticky dough forms. Turn out the dough onto a lightly floured surface. Knead until the dough is elastic, 8–10 minutes. Wrap in plastic wrap and let sit for 1 hour at room temperature.

When ready to continue, on a lightly floured surface, cut the dough into 6 pieces. Work with one piece at a time, and keep the remaining dough covered with plastic wrap. Roll dough out into long, 4-inch wide strips with a rolling pin or pasta maker. Cut into 4-inch squares. Place 2 teaspoons of filling in the middle of each square. Dampen two edges with water. Fold one corner of the dough up and over the filling to the opposite corner. Press dough to seal, squeezing out air pockets around the filling. Wrap the top corner over to the back. Fold the other two corners together, one over the other in the front, dampening them so they stick together. Transfer to a parchment paper-lined baking sheet and continue forming the tortellini.

When they are all shaped, bring a large pot of salted water to a boil. Cook tortellini until al dente, 3-4 minutes. Meanwhile, in a large skillet over medium-high heat, combine the lemon juice and zest, wine, olive oil, and black pepper. Using a slotted spoon, transfer tortellini to the skillet and cook for 2 minutes. Transfer the tortellini to a serving platter and garnish with parsley, basil, and black pepper.

Cocoa and Herb Fettuccine with Garlic Alfredo

Makes 2 to 3 Servings

Pasta di cacao (savory chocolate pasta) is a trend and one that has recently taken the food industry by storm. However, this is just the tail end of a tradition that dates back to the introduction of the cocoa bean to Italy, where it was embraced as a spice – no different from peppercorns, fennel seeds, or caraway. Particularly in Tuscany, chocolate is incorporated into many sauces, especially to accent the wild taste of game meats. We like including the chocolate flavor in the pasta dough. Try chewing on a cocoa nib and, noticing its nutty earthiness think about how that can add depth to your homemade pasta.

You can adapt this recipe to highlight your own favorite herbs in the sauce.

Fettuccini:
1 ¼ cups all-purpose flour, plus extra for flouring
¼ cup cocoa powder
3 eggs
2 teaspoons salt
1 batch **Herbed Alfredo Sauce** (see page 79)

In a large bowl, whisk together the flour and cocoa powder. Make a well in the center of this mixture. Break the eggs into the well and beat with a fork, gradually incorporating flour from the sides of the well until all the flour has been included and a sticky dough is formed.

Take the dough in your hands and knead it until it becomes smooth and elastic (3-5 minutes). Form the dough into a log shape. Cover the dough log in plastic wrap, and let sit at room temperature for at least an hour.

Cut the log into four pieces. Flatten one of the pieces with your hand or a rolling pin until it is thin enough to fit into your pasta maker. (If you don't have a pasta maker, use a rolling pin to roll out the dough until it is approximately 1/16 -inch thick, then cut into strands with a knife.) Use the pasta maker to roll out sheets that are 1/16-inch thick, then use the noodle-cutting attachment to cut the sheets into ⅛-inch strips. Repeat with the remaining pieces of dough.

Fill a large pot a little over halfway with water and bring to a boil over high heat. Add the salt. When the water has come to a rolling boil, add the pasta. Cook until al dente (around 1 minute). Drain the pasta and return it to the pot. Pour the Herbed Alfredo Sauce over the fettuccini and serve immediately.

Herbed Alfredo Sauce

1 tablespoon butter
1 clove garlic, pressed
1 cup milk
1 ½ teaspoons cornstarch
¼ cup heavy cream
1 ½ cups Parmesan cheese, freshly grated
1 teaspoon salt
1 teaspoon white pepper
¼ teaspoon nutmeg
2 teaspoons fresh rosemary needles, minced
2 teaspoons fresh basil leaves, minced
2 teaspoons fresh oregano leaves, minced
2 teaspoons fresh parsley, minced
1 teaspoon fresh thyme leaves, minced

In a medium saucepan over medium heat, melt the butter. Add the garlic and sauté for 2 minutes. Add the milk, and then the cornstarch, whisking constantly for 4 minutes or until the mixture just begins to thicken. Add the heavy cream, Parmesan cheese, salt, pepper, and nutmeg. Cook for an additional 8-10 minutes or until thickened. Remove from heat and add the rosemary, basil oregano, parsley, and thyme.

Breads

In this Chapter you will find:

Russian Black Bread

Pain au Chocolat a la Provence

Rosemary Honey Butter Rolls
with Dark Chocolate

Cranberry Sage and Blond Chocolate
Beer Bread

Thyme and Pineapple Milk Chocolate
Hawaiian Loaf

Fig and Fennel Chocolate Muffins

Russian Black Bread

Makes 1 Loaf

Russian black bread contains both unsweetened chocolate and coffee, along with caraway, fennel, and onion. It has a rich flavor that goes equally well with butter and jam or with heavy soup. Traditional black bread contains only rye flour and uses a sourdough starter, but we wanted something that would rise a bit more and have a somewhat less intense flavor. In Russian culture, bread is a symbol of friendship, is meant to be shared, and is often given away to friends.

1 tablespoon active dry yeast
¼ teaspoon sugar
¼ cup warm water (105 to 115°)
1 cup strong espresso, hot
2 tablespoons molasses
2 teaspoons brown sugar
2 tablespoons apple cider vinegar
2 tablespoons butter
1 ounce unsweetened chocolate
1 cup whole-wheat flour
1 cup dark rye flour
1 ½ cups all-purpose flour
½ tablespoon salt
¼ cup bran
1 tablespoon caraway seeds, plus ½ teaspoon, divided
½ teaspoon fennel seeds
½ tablespoon minced shallot
2 tablespoons cornmeal
2 teaspoons all-purpose flour

In a small bowl, combine yeast and sugar with warm water. Stir to dissolve and let proof, about 10 minutes.

Combine the espresso, molasses, brown sugar, apple cider vinegar, butter, and chocolate. Stir frequently until the butter and chocolate are melted. Set aside.

In a large bowl, whisk together the whole wheat flour, rye flour, all-purpose flour. Set aside.

In bowl of a stand mixer, combine two cups of the mixed flours with the salt, bran, caraway, fennel, and shallots and mix on low. Add the yeast mixture and then the espresso mixture. Continue mixing on low until the ingredients are combined, then beat at medium speed for three minutes. Return the speed to low, and pausing between additions, add half-cup measures of the remaining mixed flours until it forms a firm sticky dough (you will not need all of the mixed flours). Turn the dough out onto a floured surface and knead for 4-6 minutes until the dough becomes springy and elastic. Form into a ball and place in a greased bowl. Turn once to grease the top. Cover with plastic wrap and let rise in a warm area until doubled, about 1 ½-2 hours.

Combine the cornmeal, flour and remaining caraway seeds and set aside.

Punch down the dough. Turn out onto a lightly floured surface. Form into a round loaf and place seam down on a greased baking stone sheet. Sprinkle with the cornmeal mixture. Cover loosely with plastic wrap. Let rise until doubled and puffy, about 45 minutes to one hour. Slash an X into the top with a sharp knife.
Preheat the oven to 350°. Bake for 50 minutes or until loaves are well-browned and sound hollow inside. Remove from the baking sheet to a rack and allow to cool completely.

Pain au Chocolat a la Provence
Makes Around 9 Croissant Rolls

We stumbled across a web site once that showed pain au chocolates as "sad faces." Ever since then, we can't look at one of these sweet rolls without noticing how the twisting of the dough around two separate sticks of chocolate does indeed lend a melancholy frown. Pain au chocolat is made from the same dough as croissants, which you can shape as elegantly or as rustically as you want. We added Provence-inspired herbs to the dough. If you want to save time, you can buy herbes de Provence, an herb seasoning blend that combines many of the herbs commonly used in the Provence region. However, these "one proportion fits all" blends often contain lavender flowers, which are used only in certain dishes in Provence. For reasons such as this, we find it is often better to simply choose the herbs you want for a particular dish rather than rely on a mix with many ingredients.

¾ cup milk
1 tablespoon active dry yeast
1 ½ cups flour
1 tablespoon active dry yeast, plus 1 teaspoon
1 ¾ cups milk
6 cups flour
⅓ cup sugar
1 tablespoon salt, plus 1 teaspoon
1 tablespoon butter
1 tablespoon dried marjoram
1 tablespoon dried thyme
1 tablespoon dried savory
½ teaspoon dried sage
½ teaspoon dried basil
2 ¾ cups European-style butter
1 batch **Bittersweet Chocolate Batons** (see page 86)
4 egg yolks
¼ cup heavy cream
Pinch salt

In a small saucepan over medium heat, bring the milk to between 80 and 90 °. Pour the warmed milk into a medium bowl, and sprinkle the yeast over the milk. Stir until the yeast dissolves completely, then add the flour, mixing with a spoon until it becomes a smooth batter. Cover the bowl with a dishcloth and let the mixture (preferment) rise in a warm spot until almost double in volume (typically 2-3 hours).

Transfer the preferment to the bowl of a stand mixer fitted with a dough hook and add yeast. Mix on low speed for a minute or two until the yeast is incorporated into the preferment batter. Stop the mixer as needed and scrape down the bottom and sides of the bowl with a spatula to ensure all ingredients are evenly mixed in. When the mixture is an even and well-mixed mass, increase the speed to medium and continue to mix for a couple of minutes. Slowly add half of the milk and mix until fully incorporated.

Reduce mixer speed to low and add the flour, sugar, salt, melted butter, and remaining milk, and mix for approximately 3 minutes until a loose dough forms. Turn off the mixer and let the dough rest for 15-20 minutes. After resting, mix on low speed until the dough is smooth and elastic, a maximum of 4 minutes. If the dough is very firm, add more milk, one tablespoon at a time. Take care not to overmix the dough. You will be rolling out the dough several times, which will further develop the gluten structure. So though you want a smooth dough, the less mixing, the better. Cover the bowl with a dishcloth and allow to rise in a cool spot until the volume increases by half, approximately 1½ hours.

Lightly flour a work surface and transfer the dough. Press the dough into a rectangle 2-inches thick and wrap the rectangle in plastic or slip it into a zipper bag and seal closed. Place the dough in the refrigerator to chill for 4-6 hours.

About 30 minutes before you are ready to start laminating the dough (incorporating the butter as layers), take out the butter, unwrap, and place the sticks on a piece of waxed paper, lined up single file. Place another piece of waxed paper on top and use a rolling pin to beat and flatten the sticks into a large rectangle approximately 21 by 8-inches and ½-inch thick. Leave the butter rectangle in the waxed paper and return to the refrigerator to chill but still remain pliable.

Lightly dust a cool work surface, and then remove the chilled dough and butter from the refrigerator. Unwrap the dough and place it on the floured surface. Roll out the dough into a rectangle 28 by 12-inches.

With the long side of the rectangle facing you and starting from the left side, place the flattened rectangle of butter over two-thirds of the length of the dough rectangle. Fold the uncovered third over the butter and then fold the left-hand third over the center, as if folding a letter. The resulting rectangle is known as a plaque. Use your fingers to push down along the seams on the top and the bottom to seal the plaque.
Give the plaque a quarter turn so the seams are to your right and left, rather than at the top and bottom. Roll out the dough into a rectangle 28 by 12-inches, and fold again in the same manner as described above. Wrap the dough in plastic wrap or slip into a zipper bag and place in the refrigerator for 1½-2 hours to allow the gluten to relax before making the third turn.

Meanwhile, use a bench scraper to clean your work surface and then re-dust with flour. Remove the dough from the refrigerator, unwrap, place on the floured surface, and again roll out into a rectangle 28 by 12-inches. Fold into thirds in the same manner described above to complete the third turn. Wrap the dough in plastic wrap or slip into a zipper bag and place in the freezer to chill for at least 1 hour. If you intend to make the croissants the next morning, leave the dough in the freezer until the evening and then transfer it to the refrigerator before going to bed. The next morning, the dough will be ready to roll out and form, proof, and bake. The dough can be frozen for up to 1 week; transfer it to the refrigerator to thaw overnight before using.

When you are ready to roll out the dough, dust the work surface with flour again. For the pain au chocolat, cut 8 by 4-inch rectangles of dough and place a baton at each short end. Roll the dough around each one toward the center and place face down on the pan.

When ready to bake, place a pan of steaming water on the bottom rack of the oven (turned off) and set the pastry pan(s) on the middle rack for approximately 2-3 hours to allow the dough to proof. Refresh the pan of water halfway through the rising to ensure that no skin forms on the pastries.

During this final rise, the croissants and rolls should at least double in size and look noticeably puffy. Test for doneness by pressing a roll or croissant lightly with a fingertip – if the indentation fills in slowly, they are almost ready to bake. When ready, remove the pans from the oven and set the oven to 425° to preheat for 20-30 minutes.

About 10 minutes before the oven is ready, mix up the egg wash. In a small bowl, whisk together the egg yolks, cream, and salt until you have a pale yellow mixture. Using a pastry brush, lightly and carefully brush the yolk mixture on the pastries, being careful not to allow the egg wash to drip onto the pan. Let the wash dry slightly before baking.

Place the sheet pans of croissants and rolls into the oven and turn the oven temperature down to 400°. Leave the door shut for the first 10 minutes and then, working quickly, open the oven door, rotate the pan(s) 180°, and close the door. This will allow the pastries to bake evenly. Bake for 6-10 minutes longer, rotating the pan again during this time if the rolls and croissants do not appear to be baking evenly. The croissants and rolls should be fully baked within a total of 15-20 minutes. They should be a deep golden to almost dark brown on the top and bottom, crisp on the outside, and feel light when picked up, indicating that the interior is cooked through.

Remove the pastries from the oven and transfer to a wire rack to cool. As they cool, their moist interiors will set up. They are best if eaten while they are still slightly warm.

Bittersweet Chocolate Batons

8 ounces bittersweet chocolate, tempered (see page 17)

Pour the warm tempered chocolate into 4-inch long stick shapes on waxed paper. If this feels too messy, cut stick-shapes from a bar of chocolate.

Herbie Info Box

Savory is actually a very versatile herb. Though its name connotes something that is not sweet, savory was used during the middle ages to add a complimentary note of spice to pies and cakes. If you purchase dried savory for this recipe and are stumped for other ways to use it, look to the Atlantic Canadian culinary kitchen, which treats savory the way other cultures treat sage – as an herb indispensable in chicken dishes and ground pork.

There are two varieties of savory. In most culinary traditions, summer savory is the preferable variety. Summer savory is a fast-growing herb that can be harvested continually throughout its growing season. At the end of the season, you can harvest the whole plant and dry it for use in recipes like this where the dried herb works better.

Rosemary Honey Butter Roll with Dark Chocolate

Makes 13 Rolls

Rosemary and chocolate are two of our favorite flavors. They come together beautifully in these rolls. The cheese gives an added richness, but you won't necessarily notice it as a separate flavor. Choose a light-flavored honey. You don't need much for this recipe, but don't worry. Honey is the only food that never expires. Archeologists have unearthed honey from 3,000 year old Egyptian tombs and found it edible. Surely yours won't be on the shelf that long. If it crystalizes, place the container in a bowl of warm water and stir it.

You can adapt this recipe to highlight your own favorite herbs in the sauce.

Olive oil, for greasing
1 ½ cups all-purpose flour, plus additional as needed and for flouring
3 tablespoons sugar
2 teaspoons active dry yeast
1 teaspoon salt
¾ cup warm water (105 to 115°)
2 tablespoons butter, plus 1 tablespoon, melted, divided
¾ cup shredded Colby Jack cheese
1 teaspoon fresh rosemary, minced
3 ounces dark chocolate, chopped
2 teaspoons honey

Grease a 9-inch round baking pan.

In the bowl of a mixer, combine the flour, sugar, yeast, and salt and blend together on low. Add the water and 2 tablespoons butter. Beat on medium speed for 3 minutes or until smooth. Stir in the cheese and rosemary. Add enough additional flour to form a soft dough.

Turn onto a lightly floured surface and knead until smooth and elastic, about 4-6 minutes. Add the chocolate and knead a few more times to incorporate. Lightly oil the bowl. Return dough to bowl. Cover with a dish towel and let rest for 10 minutes. Divide into 13 pieces. Shape each into a ball. Place in prepared baking pan. Cover and let rise in a warm place until doubled, about 30 minutes.

Preheat oven to 375°. Bake 11-14 minutes or until lightly browned.

Combine the honey and remaining butter and brush over rolls. Let cool.

Cranberry Sage and Blond Chocolate Beer Bread

Makes 1 Loaf

Blond chocolate can be hard to track down, but it is worth the effort. It's like eating white chocolate and caramel in the same bite. Those caramel notes blend perfectly with the tartness of the cranberry and the peppery element in the sage. If you can't find caramelized white chocolate locally and you don't want to wait for it to ship, you can substitute white chocolate.

3 cups all-purpose flour
1 ½ tablespoons baking powder
1 ½ teaspoons salt
½ cup sugar
2 tablespoons dried sage (1 tablespoon for a subtle flavor)
12 ounces beer
1 cup fresh or frozen cranberries
1 cup chopped walnuts
½ cup blond (caramelized) white chocolate, chopped
2 tablespoons melted butter

Preheat the oven to 375°. Butter a loaf pan and set aside.

In the bowl of a mixer, combine the flour, baking powder, salt, sugar, and sage. Mix on low speed to combine. Add the beer and mix on medium speed until a sticky dough forms. Add the cranberries, walnuts, and white chocolate and mix until just combined. Pour the dough into the loaf pan and bake for 55 minutes. At the last 3 minutes of baking, remove from the oven, brush the top of the loaf with honey butter, and return it to the oven. Cool for 5 minutes before removing from pan.

Thyme and Pineapple Milk Chocolate Hawaiian Loaf

Makes 1 Loaf

Hawaiian bread is already slightly sweet, so the milk chocolate melted into this batter feels right at home. The thyme adds a bright, almost citrusy note. Don't substitute fresh pineapple for the dried – it will make the dough soggy.

½ cup milk, warmed
1 tablespoon active dry yeast
½ teaspoon sugar, plus ½ cup, divided
½ cup evaporated milk
3 tablespoons butter
Pinch nutmeg
1 teaspoon lemon zest
4 cups all-purpose flour
4 eggs, lightly beaten, plus 1 egg, beaten, for glaze
1 teaspoon salt
½ cup milk chocolate, melted and cooled
½ cup dried pineapple, finely chopped
½ cup macadamia nuts, roughly chopped
3 tablespoons fresh thyme leaves, chopped

Mix the milk, ½ teaspoon sugar and yeast. Set aside and allow to proof for 10-15 minutes.

In a saucepan, warm the evaporated milk. Add the butter, nutmeg, sugar, and lemon zest. Stir until the butter is melted. Set aside.

Place the flour in the bowl of a mixer. Add the eggs, yeast mixture, and salt and mix on medium-low speed until combined. Add just enough of the evaporated milk mixture to form a soft dough (you may not need all of it). Add the melted chocolate, pineapple, macadamia nuts, and thyme. Knead for eight minutes or until the dough is springy, then form it into a ball. Oil a large bowl and place the dough inside. Cover the bowl with cling wrap and place in a warm spot. Allow the loaf to rise to double its size, usually about an hour.

Punch the dough down, then let it rise again. Form into a round loaf and allow to rise one more time.

Preheat the oven to 325°. Mix the egg with 1 tablespoon of water and brush it on top of the loaf. Bake in the preheated oven for about 50 minutes.

Fig and Fennel Chocolate Muffins
Makes Around 18 Muffins

Fennel bulbs walk a fine line between an herb and a vegetable (parts of it are sometimes sautéed in Mediterranean-style vegetable medleys). In this recipe, the bulb is shredded to create the structure of the muffin (think carrot cake, but with a smoother finished texture). The bulb is the mildest part of this herb, so you may like it even if you aren't a fan of fennel seeds.

For a stronger herbal flavor, add a teaspoon or two of fennel seeds and a teaspoon of celery seed to the batter before baking. We love the way the flavors of fig and fennel complement each other. And, of course, the chocolate chunks add a feeling of decadence.

2 ½ cups flour
3 tablespoons cocoa powder
2 teaspoons baking powder
½ teaspoon salt
2 cups fennel bulb, shredded
2 eggs
⅓ cup vegetable oil
⅓ cup milk
¾ cup brown sugar
1 teaspoon vanilla
4 ounces semisweet chocolate, chopped
¾ cup dried mission figs, chopped

Preheat the oven to 400°. Grease a 12-cup muffin tin.

In a large bowl, whisk together the flour, cocoa powder, baking powder, and salt. In a separate bowl, combine the eggs, vegetable, oil, milk, brown sugar, and vanilla and whisk until well combined. Add the shredded fennel to the egg mixture and stir in well. Add the flour mixture to the egg mixture and stir just until the dry ingredients are incorporated. Add the chopped chocolate and the figs and stir briefly. Spoon the batter into the prepared muffin tin, filling the cups ⅔ full. Bake for 20 minutes or until the muffins are springy. Allow to cool in the pan for 5 minutes, then turn out onto a wire rack to cool completely.

Ice Cream

In this Chapter you will find:

Chocolate Mint and Matcha Ice Cream

**Lavender Honey Ice Cream
with Dark Chocolate Chunks**

Cocoa Nib, Cinnamon and Bay Ice Cream

Blackberry and Sage Chocolate Gelato

Lemongrass White Chocolate Coconut Gelato

Chocolate Mint and Matcha Ice Cream

Makes 1 (32-ounce) Container

We like incorporating tea in foods, as they are an easy way to add a strong dose of flavor without unduly changing the texture. Unlike most teas, Japanese matcha is finely ground and intended to be dissolved into the steeping medium. This makes it ideal for dyeing foods a beautiful mint green color. Perhaps this is what put us in mind of combining the green tea flavor with mint. Mint was common in ancient Japan, and minty flavor elements are not uncommon in modern day Japan.

Chocolate mint rounds out the white chocolate here, but you could use the mint of your choice – or you could even use green shiso, a uniquely Japanese member of the mint family which reminds many of basil, mint, or cinnamon.

- **2 tablespoons matcha powder**
- **6 tablespoons hot water**
- **1 ½ cups milk**
- **5-6 sprigs chocolate mint**
- **4 egg yolks**
- **10 tablespoons sugar**
- **8 ounces white chocolate, chopped**
- **1 ½ cups heavy cream, whipped**

Combine the matcha powder and the hot water in a small bowl and set aside. In a medium saucepan, combine the milk and the chocolate mint sprigs over medium heat. Bring the mixture just to the boiling point, then remove the saucepan from the heat, cover, and allow to steep for at least 20 minutes.

Combine the egg yolks and sugar in a saucepan and whisk until combined. Add the milk to the pan in a steady stream while whisking constantly. Add the white chocolate and place the pan over medium-low heat. Continue whisking constantly until the mixture has thickened. Remove the pan from the heat to an ice water bath. Add the matcha tea paste, whisking it into the mixture until uniform. When the mixture has cooled completely, fold in the whipped heavy cream. Pour the mixture into an ice cream maker and freeze according to the manufacturer's directions. Transfer the soft ice cream to a lidded container. Allow to harden for at least 3-4 hours before serving.

Lavender Honey Ice Cream with Dark Chocolate Chunks

Makes 1 (32-ounce) Container

It can be fun to combine different herbs to create a rounded flavor. But sometimes you just want to experience the pure flavor of a single herb layered with itself in different forms. In this ice cream, we combined steeped lavender flowers with lavender honey. For an even stronger lavender element, a couple of teaspoons of lavender flowers can be finely ground and added to the strained ice cream base (though some find really strong lavender flavors "soapy"). Lavender is one of those herbs that it is easy to become obsessed with. Just look at Queen Victoria, who used it in her teapot, in her clothing drawers, and just about anywhere else – including having the floors and walls of her home washed with lavender.

Victoria also endorsed chocolate. In December of 1899, she sent a gift of chocolate packaged in a tin bearing her likeness to each of her soldiers in South Africa in an attempt to raise morale. While it was an unpopular move at the time, the tins are still considered collector's items. We imagine she would have approved of this ice cream.

4 ounces bittersweet chocolate
2 tablespoons steeped lavender tea
2 cups heavy cream
1 cup half-and-half
⅔ cup Lavender-Infused Honey (see page 147)
2 tablespoons food-grade lavender flowers
2 eggs
⅛ teaspoon salt

Chop the chocolate and place into a double boiler over barely simmering water. Add the lavender tea and melt the chocolate, stirring frequently. When smooth, pour the chocolate onto a baking sheet lined with parchment paper. Place the baking sheet in the freezer and freeze until the chocolate becomes firm. Chop the chocolate into chunks and return to the freezer until needed.

Bring cream, half-and-half, honey, and lavender just to a boil in a 2-quart heavy saucepan over moderate heat, stirring occasionally, then remove pan from heat. Let steep, covered, for 30 minutes.

Pour cream mixture through a fine-mesh sieve into a bowl and discard the lavender. Return the mixture to the cleaned saucepan over medium heat. Heat through.

Whisk together eggs and salt in a large bowl, then add 1 cup hot cream mixture in a slow stream while whisking constantly. Add egg mixture to the saucepan and simmer, stirring constantly, until mixture thickens (at 170-180°).

Remove the saucepan from the heat and transfer to a cold-water bath until chilled.

Pour into an ice cream maker and freeze according to the manufacturer's directions. When it is almost frozen, add the chocolate chunks. Transfer the soft ice cream to a lidded container. Allow to harden for at least 3 to 4 hours before serving.

Cocoa Nib, Cinnamon and Bay Ice Cream

Makes 1 (32-ounce) Container

When using most herbs, we prefer the fresh version. However, fresh bay leaves are but a shadow of their future selves, as the typical bay flavor does not develop fully until several weeks after the leaves have been dried. We find it interesting that bay laurel and cinnamon are both lauraceas (members of the laurel family). This makes it a little less surprising how well the leaf of a tree native to the Mediterranean complements the bark of a tree that is native to Sri Lanka and Indonesia. Laurels were used to fashion the crowns given to poets and heroes in ancient Greece as well as to other people of status. If you want to reward yourself or show someone how important they are to you, give this ice cream a try. We also love the way the cocoa nibs here feel like a cross between chocolate chips and nuts.

1 ½ cups heavy cream
1 ½ cups whole milk
¼ cup cocoa nibs, plus 3 tablespoons
3 (3-inch) cinnamon sticks, crushed
2 bay leaves
½ cup sugar
⅛ teaspoon salt

Combine the heavy cream, milk, ¼ cup cocoa nibs, cinnamon sticks, bay leaves, sugar, and salt in a medium saucepan over medium heat, stirring frequently until the sugar melts. Bring the mixture to a boil, then remove the saucepan from the heat. Cover the saucepan and let the liquid steep for half an hour. Strain the mixture (discarding solids) into the chamber of an ice cream maker and freeze according to the manufacturer's direction. Add the 3 tablespoon cocoa nibs near the end of the freezing process. Transfer the soft ice cream to a lidded container. Harden for at least three to four hours before serving.

Blackberry and Sage Chocolate Gelato

Makes 1 (32-ounce) Container

It is hard to find a more refreshing combination than sweet blackberry and peppery sage, which is perhaps why it is so often used in teas, lemonades and flavored waters. When we decided to blend this already complex mixture with a rich chocolate gelato, we didn't want the more delicate sage to get lost among all the bold, rich flavors surrounding it, so we included sage in both the ice cream base and the raspberry swirl. Sage is a common name used for a number of plants, not all of which are suitable for culinary use. Make sure you are using salvia officinalis (usually called garden sage or common sage), which has a number of cultivars (all of which are suitable for use in this ice cream).

1 cup blackberries
½ cup powdered sugar
2 cups whole milk
⅔ cup heavy cream
½ cup sugar, plus ¼ cup, divided
20 fresh sage leaves, plus 3 minced
8 - 9 lemon thyme sprigs
1 cup cocoa powder
2 ounces bittersweet chocolate
4 egg yolks
2 teaspoons vanilla
⅛ teaspoon salt

Combine the blackberries, the minced sage leaves, and the powdered sugar in a medium saucepan over medium heat. Bring to a simmer, stirring frequently. Continue to simmer for 10 minutes. Set aside to cool.

Heat the milk, cream, and ½ cup of sugar over a medium heat until the sugar dissolves and the mixture starts to simmer. Add the cocoa powder and bittersweet chocolate and whisk until smooth. Remove the saucepan from the heat. Stir in the 20 sage leaves and allow the mixture to steep for at least 20 minutes.

In a mixing bowl, whisk together the egg yolks and the remaining ¼ cup of sugar. Slowly add in 1 cup of the hot milk mixture, pouring in a steady stream while whisking continuously. Pour the egg mixture into the saucepan and cook over a medium low heat until thickened (170-180°).

Remove from the heat and transfer to an ice water bath. Add the vanilla and salt and stir to combine. When completely cool, pour the mixture through a strainer into an ice cream maker. Freeze according to the manufacturer's directions.

Transfer the soft gelato and the raspberry mixture in alternating layers to a lidded container (⅓ of the gelato followed by ⅓ of the blackberry mixture – you may not need to add all of the liquid from the blackberries). Allow to harden for at least 3-4 hours before serving.

Herbie Info Box

Sage can be a difficult herb to grow. It hates to get its feet wet, so if you live in an area with heavy or unpredictable rainfall, you might consider growing it in a container. We tend to favor the variegated cultivars such as this one simply because we find they offer visual interest in the garden. When harvesting sage, don't take the entire branch off the plant, but rather, just trim a few individual leaves. It is also better if you take the leaves from different locations on the plant, rather than stripping a single branch.

Lemongrass White Chocolate Coconut Gelato

Makes 1 (32-ounce) Container

Lemongrass is one of our favorite herbs. It grows as a practically maintenance-free ornamental grass but delivers a punch of citrusy flavor. The blade of the grass grows tall, but the part usually used is the base of the stem (where it is round and spirals in on itself). Make sure to smash the stalks with the side of your knife in order to release the plant oils. Lemongrass is native to Asia, and it is an essential part of Thai cooking. We've adapted a traditional Thai-style coconut milk gelato to highlight the lemony flavor, using white chocolate to add depth and intensity to the finished gelato. Both gelatin and cornstarch clump very easily, so it is critically important to keep stirring while cooking the ice cream base.

2 (13.5-ounce) cans coconut milk
4 ounces white chocolate, chopped
4 to 6 stems lemongrass, smashed
2 teaspoons unflavored gelatin powder
2 tablespoons cornstarch
1 cup nonfat dry milk
¾ cup sugar
⅛ teaspoon salt
Dry-roasted peanuts, for garnish

Place the coconut milk, white chocolate and lemongrass in a medium saucepan over medium-high heat. Stir frequently until the chocolate melts. Stirring constantly, add the gelatin and cornstarch. Add the dry milk, sugar and salt, then bring the mixture to a gentle boil, still stirring constantly. Once the sugar and gelatin have dissolved, remove the pot from the heat and place in an ice bath. When it has cooled completely, remove the lemongrass stalks and transfer the mixture to an ice cream maker. Freeze the mixture according to the manufacturer's instructions. Transfer the soft ice cream to a lidded container. Allow to harden for at least 3-4 hours before serving. Garnish each bowl with the roasted peanuts.

Pour cream mixture through a fine-mesh sieve into a bowl and discard the lavender. Return the mixture to the cleaned saucepan over medium heat. Heat through.

Whisk together eggs and salt in a large bowl, then add 1 cup hot cream mixture in a slow stream while whisking constantly. Add egg mixture to the saucepan and simmer, stirring constantly, until mixture thickens (at 170-180°).

Remove the saucepan from the heat and transfer to a cold-water bath until chilled.

Pour into an ice cream maker and freeze according to the manufacturer's directions. When it is almost frozen, add the chocolate chunks. Transfer the soft ice cream to a lidded container. Allow to harden for at least 3 to 4 hours before serving.

Cookies and Bars

In this Chapter you will find:

Mint Chocolate Chip Cookies

Lavender Cocoa Nib Shortbread Cookies

Chocolate Lavender Madeleines

White Chocolate Coconut Lime Cookies with Cilantro

Thymely Chocolate Grapefruit Meringues

Chocolate Gingerbread

Ginger Mint Brownies

Mint Chocolate Chip Cookies

Makes 2 Dozen Cookies

Mint and chocolate are a popular combination for dessert flavors, but they often taste quite artificial. This is a back-to-basics chocolate chip cookie recipe – with dried mint added to give a subtle, natural flavor. Mint from the grocery store produce section is almost always spearmint. You can experiment using dried peppermint or any of the flavored mint varieties, such as orange mint, cinnamon mint, or chocolate mint.

21 tablespoon dried mint leaves
2 cups all-purpose flour
1 teaspoon baking soda
½ teaspoon salt
½ cup sugar
½ cup dark brown sugar
½ cup butter, at room temperature
1 teaspoon vanilla
1 egg
½ cup chocolate chips

Preheat oven to 350°.

Process the mint in a spice grinder until it forms a powder.
In a medium bowl, whisk together the flour, baking soda, salt, and mint.

In the bowl of a mixer, cream together the sugar, brown sugar, and butter. Add the vanilla and egg and beat on medium-low speed until combined. As three separate additions, add the flour mixture, combining well between each. Stir in the chocolate chips.

Scoop the dough into 2-inch balls onto baking sheets and bake for 18 minutes.

Lavender Cocoa Nib Shortbread Cookies

Makes 2 Dozen Cookies

Lavender shortbread is an herb gardener's classic, highlighting the floral flavor of lavender in a cookie that has wide appeal. It's our go-to for encouraging people to try adding herbal flavors to their culinary repertoire. When cocoa nibs are added, it presents an opportunity to present a less familiar form of chocolate as well.

22 teaspoons dried lavender blossoms
⅔ cup sugar
2 teaspoons lemon zest
1 cup butter, softened
2 cups all-purpose flour
½ teaspoon salt
¼ cup cocoa nibs

Preheat the oven to 350°.

Combine the lavender blossoms and a tablespoon of the sugar in a spice grinder and process until the flowers are powdered. In a medium bowl, combine the powdered lavender, remaining sugar, and lemon zest. Set aside.

In a separate bowl, whisk together the flour, salt, and cocoa nibs. Set aside.

Cream together the sugar mixture and the butter in the bowl of a stand mixer. Add the flour mixture and beat on low until a soft dough forms. Transfer the dough to a sheet of waxed paper and refrigerate for 20 minutes. Form the dough into two 4-inch logs and chill for at least 45 additional minutes.

Slice the shortbread dough into 1/4-inch thick rounds and place the rounds on ungreased baking sheets.

Bake the shortbread for 20-25 minutes or until the edges are lightly browned. Transfer the baked shortbread to a wire rack to cool completely.

Chocolate Lavender Madeleines

Makes Around 16 Servings

Madeleines, those lemony butter cakes that were first enjoyed in the Lorraine region of France and later remembered in poetic form by Proust, require a special pan, which is shaped as an elongated seashell. While you can pour this butter sponge batter into an ordinary muffin tin, it won't be as special. And it won't really be a Madeline. We wanted to keep the flavors of the original, imparted by the melted butter and the lemon, while adding that most French herb, lavender, along with the richness of dark chocolate. There are a number of conflicting stories detailing exactly how the Madeline came about. One proposes that a girl named Madeline made the cookies for the Duke of Lorraine, who in turn gave some of the treats to his daughter, Marie, who happened to be the wife of Louis XV. And with courtly favor, the popularity of the Madeleine could not help but grow.

½ cup butter, plus extra for greasing
1 teaspoon lavender flowers, plus extra for sprinkling
3 ½ ounces dark chocolate
2 eggs
1 cup lavender-**Scented Sugar** (see page 148)
1 teaspoon lemon zest
1 cup cake flour
1 teaspoon baking powder

Melt the butter in a small saucepan over medium heat. Remove from heat and allow to cool a little. When it stops sizzling, add the lavender flowers and allow this mixture to steep for at least 30 minutes. Meanwhile, melt the chocolate in a double boiler over barely simmering water. Remove the chocolate from the heat. Pour the butter through a sieve (discarding solids) into the chocolate and whisk to combine.

Preheat the oven to 425°. Grease the Madeleine molds. Cream the eggs and sugar together until light and creamy. Add the lemon zest, flour, and baking powder. Mix well. Add the chocolate and stir to incorporate. Sprinkle a few dried lavender flowers into the bottom of each mold. Spoon the batter into the molds (they should be about two-thirds full). Bake for 5 minutes, then reduce the oven temperature to 350° and bake for an additional 8-10 minutes. Remove the molds from the oven and let cool for 5 minutes. Turn the Madelines out on a wire rack and cool completely.

White Chocolate Coconut Lime Cookies with Cilantro

Makes 3 Dozen Cookies

Cilantro goes by many names, including coriander (though this name is sometimes reserved exclusively for the plant's seeds) and Chinese parsley. It is native to various regions throughout the world (including Spain) and is used extensively in any number of cultural kitchens – including Mexico. We were once discussing how well cilantro pairs with lime in Mexican cuisine, then how well lime pairs with coconut, and then how well coconut pairs with chocolate. The result of our musings was this white chocolate-studded cookie. Don't worry – it's not a "salsa cookie." The cilantro just gives the cookie an almost indefinable "something" which all of our test tasters really enjoyed.

1 ¼ cups all-purpose flour
½ teaspoon baking soda
¼ teaspoon salt
½ cup butter
½ cup dark brown sugar
½ cup sugar
2 teaspoons cilantro, finely minced
3-4 kaffir lime leaves, finely minced
2 teaspoons lime juice
1 teaspoon lime zest
1 egg
1 ½ cups flaked coconut
1 ½ cups white chocolate chunks

Preheat oven to 350°. Line baking sheets with parchment paper.

In a medium bowl, whisk together the flour, baking soda, and salt.

In a large bowl, cream together the butter with both sugars until light and fluffy. Add the cilantro, kaffir lime leaves, lime juice and zest and egg, and beat until completely incorporated. Gradually blend in the flour mixture, then mix in the coconut and white chocolate. Roll the dough into 1-inch balls and place three inches apart on the prepared baking sheets. Bake for 8-10 minutes. Allow to cool in the pan for 5 minutes, then transfer the cookies to a wire rack and allow to cool completely.

Thymely Chocolate Grapefruit Meringues

Makes 4 Dozen Meringues

Meringues are often served when a host or hostess is looking for a lower calorie option for dessert. We took this healthy impulse and infused it with chocolate and grapefruit. These flavors are also combined in traditional European-style candied citrus peels, which we took as our inspiration, and as a result, this meringue contains a good dose of grapefruit zest. The grapefruit zest takes on a caramelized taste as it cooks in its own juice and achieves a chewy texture that adds a bit of interest to the finished meringue. The thyme leaves heighten the flavor. It may be tempting to skip a step and add the grapefruit juice directly to the whipped egg whites, but adding liquid to the eggs will make them runny and ruin your meringues.

6 ounces bittersweet chocolate, chopped
1 tablespoon grapefruit zest
½ cup grapefruit juice
2 teaspoons thyme leaves, minced
2 egg whites, at room temperature
⅛ teaspoon cream of tartar
¼ cup powdered sugar

Combine the grapefruit juice and zest with the minced thyme leaves in the top of a double boiler. Set this pan directly on the burner over medium heat and cook, stirring frequently, until the liquid has reduced by a little over half. Place the double boiler top onto its bottom half (filled with an inch or so of barely simmering water). Melt the chocolate into the grapefruit mixture, stirring frequently, until the mixture is smooth. Set aside to cool.

Preheat the oven to 280°. Line a baking sheet with parchment paper. In a large bowl, combine the egg whites and the cream of tartar and whip until soft peaks form. Add the sugar, and continue whipping the egg whites until stiff peaks form. Gently fold in the melted chocolate mixture. Spoon the mixture into a pastry bag fitted with a large star tip and squeeze gently to make "kiss" shapes. Bake for 20 minutes. Increase the temperature to 300° and bake for an additional 10-15 minutes. If the meringues aren't dry to the touch, turn oven down to 200° and prop the door open until the meringues are done. Transfer to an airtight container.

Chocolate Gingerbread
Makes 1 (9 x 11-inch) Pan

We kept all the traditional flavors of gingerbread in this version, which we infused with chocolate liquor. This one was a favorite with our taste testers, because it amps up the ginger and orange so you can still taste it alongside the chocolate. We find that mini chocolate chips are less disruptive to the traditional gingerbread texture than standard chocolate chips.

½ cup butter
½ cup sugar
1 egg
2 ½ cups all-purpose flour, sifted, measured after sifting
1 ½ teaspoons baking soda
2 ½ teaspoons cinnamon
2 ½ teaspoons ginger
½ teaspoon salt
½ cup light molasses
½ cup honey
½ cup chocolate liqueur
½ cup hot water
2 tablespoons **Candied Orange Peel** (see page 146)
1 teaspoon fresh orange zest
½ cup mini chocolate chips

Preheat oven to 350°. Grease a 9 x 11-inch pan.

Melt the butter and set aside to cool.

In a large bowl, whisk together the flour, baking soda, cinnamon, ginger, and salt.

In a separate bowl, combine the molasses, honey, chocolate liqueur, hot water, candied orange peel, and orange zest.

Transfer the melted butter to the bowl of a mixer. Add the sugar and egg and beat well. Add the sifted and liquid ingredients alternately to the egg mixture, blending on medium-low speed until well combined. Gently stir in mini chocolate chips. Pour into the prepared pan and bake for approximately 1 hour or until a toothpick comes out clean when inserted into the center of the gingerbread.

Ginger Mint Brownies
Makes 1 (11 x 13-inch) Pan

We wanted to create a brownie that celebrated the flavors of Southeast Asia, one of our favorite culinary regions. We kept thinking about a citrusy ginger mint dressing popular in Malaysian/Thai cuisine (usually served with a good dose of peanut) and how well it represents certain aspects of the cuisine. We incorporated the various flavors into the layers of this brownie, which has a ginger/peanut base, a mint frosting, and a citrus glaze. A number of the steps have you putting this in the refrigerator, but the flavors don't really come together properly until you allow the finished dessert to come to room temperature.

Brownie Layer:
1 cup sugar
1 cup dark brown sugar
1 cup butter, softened
4 eggs
3-inch finger of ginger
4 ounces unsweetened chocolate
2 ½ cups all-purpose flour
¼ teaspoon salt
¼ teaspoon baking powder
2 teaspoons vanilla
1 cup dry-roasted peanuts

Frosting Layer:
½ cup chocolate mint or orange mint leaves
1 ¾ cups powdered sugar, plus 4 tablespoon, divided
4 tablespoons butter, softened
2 tablespoons coconut milk

Glaze Layer:
6 tablespoons butter
1 cup bittersweet chocolate, chopped
2 teaspoons powdered ginger
1 ½ teaspoons sweet orange zest

For the brownie layer:
Grease a 9 x 13-inch pan. Preheat oven to 325°.

Melt the unsweetened chocolate in a double boiler over barely simmering water. Set aside to cool.

In a small bowl, whisk together the flour, salt, and baking powder. In large bowl, cream the sugar and butter together until it becomes fluffy. Add the eggs and vanilla and beat until well blended. Roughly peel the ginger and cut into chunks that will fit in a garlic press. Press the juice and pulp into the egg and butter mixture. Add the melted chocolate and stir well to combine. Add the flour mixture to the egg mixture and stir well. Spread the batter into the prepared pan and bake for 30-35 minutes or until a toothpick inserted into the brownies comes out clean. Transfer to a wire rack and allow the brownie layer to cool completely in the pan.

For the frosting layer:
Using a mortar and pestle, grind together the mint leaves and the 4 tablespoons of powdered sugar until they form a smooth paste. Transfer this paste to a large bowl and add the remaining powdered sugar along with the butter and milk. Beat this mixture until creamy, then spread the frosting onto the brownie layer.

For the glaze layer:
Combine the butter and the bittersweet chocolate in a double boiler over barely simmering water. Stir frequently until the chocolate melts and the mixture is smooth. Remove the pan from the heat and stir in the powdered ginger and orange zest. Allow the glaze to cool, then pour it gently over frosting layer, using a spoon to spread it into the corners. Refrigerate until the glaze has solidified. Allow the brownies to soften slightly before cutting into squares.

Cakes, Puddings and Pies

In this Chapter you will find:

Chartreuse Black Forest Cake

**Chocolate Cinnamon Cupcakes
with Lemongrass Frosting**

Rose Geranium Chocolate Pound Cake

Violet Chocolate Cheesecake

**Chocolate Pear Tart
with Herbed Sweet Dough Crust**

Jasmine Liqueur Chocoflan

Lemon Verbena Chocolate Crème Brulee

Cocoa Masala Chai Soufflés

**Espresso Tamarind White Chocolate Mousse
with Clove Whipped Cream**

Chartreuse Black Forest Cake

Makes 1 (3-layer, 8-inch) Cake

We infused the batter of this cake with Chartreuse. Like many herbal liqueurs, Chartreuse was originally medicinal. According to tradition, François Hannibal d'Estrées, a marshal of artillery to French King Henry IV, brought an alchemical manuscript with a recipe for an "elixir of long life" to the Carthusian monks at Vauvert, near Paris, in 1605. After the manuscript reached the headquarters at the Grande Chartreuse monastery in Voiron, near Grenoble, it began to be used to produce the "Elixir Végétal de la Grande Chartreuse." It is such an intense green color that chartreuse green is actually named for it. If you can't find Chartreuse, substitute your favorite herbal liqueur.

1 ¼ cups butter, plus extra for greasing
8 ounces dark chocolate, chopped
2 cups all-purpose flour
1 ¾ cups sugar
¼ cup cocoa powder
1 teaspoon baking soda
¼ teaspoon salt
2 medium eggs
¾ cup buttermilk
½ cup Chartreuse (or other herbal liqueur)
1 (15-ounce) can pitted cherries, plus 2 tablespoon juice reserved
4 tablespoons kirsch
½ cup cherry preserves
2 cups heavy whipping cream
5 ounces semisweet chocolate, chopped
1 teaspoon Chartreuse
3 tablespoons powdered sugar
1 cup fresh cherries

Heat oven to 350°. Grease and line the base of three 8-inch cake pans.

Put the butter and dark chocolate in a small pan and gently heat, stirring, until completely melted. Set aside.

Whisk together the flour, sugar, cocoa, baking soda, and salt in the bowl of a stand mixer.

In a separate bowl, whisk the eggs, buttermilk, and Chartreuse together and pour into the flour mixture. Add the melted chocolate mixture and mix on low until incorporated.

Divide the mixture between the pans and bake for 25 minutes or until a toothpick comes out clean.

Prick the cakes a few times with a skewer. Mix together the reserved cherry juice and the Kirsch and drizzle over the cakes. Cool the cakes completely.

In a small bowl, stir together the drained cherries and cherry preserves. Set aside.

In a small pan, heat ¾ cup of the cream just to the simmering point. Remove from heat. Add the semisweet chocolate and stir until melted. Stir in the 1 teaspoon Chartreuse. Set aside until completely cooled.
In the bowl of a mixer, beat the remaining 1 ¼ cups cream and the powdered sugar together until stiff peaks form.

Place one of the cakes on a stable base. Spread half of the whipped cream over the top of it, and top the whipped cream with half of the jam mixture. Place the second cake on top of the first cake, and repeat the layering of the whipped cream and jam. Place the third cake on the top. Pour the ganache over the top of cake. Decorate the top and base of the cake with the fresh cherries..

Chocolate Cinnamon Cupcakes with Lemongrass Frosting

Makes 24 Cupcakes

The frosting for these cupcakes combines cinnamon whiskey with lemongrass-infused butter. The cinnamon hits you first – and then the lemon comes in as a back note. Lemongrass is too gritty and abrasive to mince into a baked good, and you don't want to add too much liquid to a frosting, so do take the time to infuse the butter and cool it back to a solid. For a nonalcoholic version, add two teaspoons of cinnamon to the frosting, and add milk to replace the missing liquid.

1 cup cocoa powder
2 cups hot coffee
2 ⅔ cups all-purpose flour
4 teaspoons baking powder
2 tablespoons cinnamon
½ teaspoon salt
1 cup butter, at room temperature
2 cups sugar
4 eggs
2 teaspoons vanilla
1 batch Lemongrass Buttercream Frosting (see page 117)

Preheat oven to 375°. Line two 12-cup cupcake pans with paper wrappers.

Combine the cocoa powder and the hot coffee in a medium bowl. Stir to dissolve. Set aside and allow to cool to room temperature.
In a large bowl, combine the flour, baking powder, cinnamon, and salt.

In the bowl of a mixer, cream the butter and sugar, then add the eggs and vanilla. Mix well. Add the flour mixture and mix until just combined. Stir in the chocolate mixture and mix to a uniform color.

Scoop two tablespoons of batter into each paper cup. Bake for 15-18 minutes. Allow to cool completely, then frost with Lemongrass Buttercream Frosting.

Lemongrass Buttercream Frosting

1 batch Lemongrass-Infused Butter (see page 145)
Shortening, as needed
4 cups sifted confectioners' sugar
4 tablespoons cinnamon whiskey

Measure the lemongrass butter, and add enough shortening to total one cup.

In the bowl of a stand mixer, cream the butter. Gradually add the sugar, one cup at a time, beating well on medium speed. Add the cinnamon whiskey and beat at medium speed until light and fluffy.

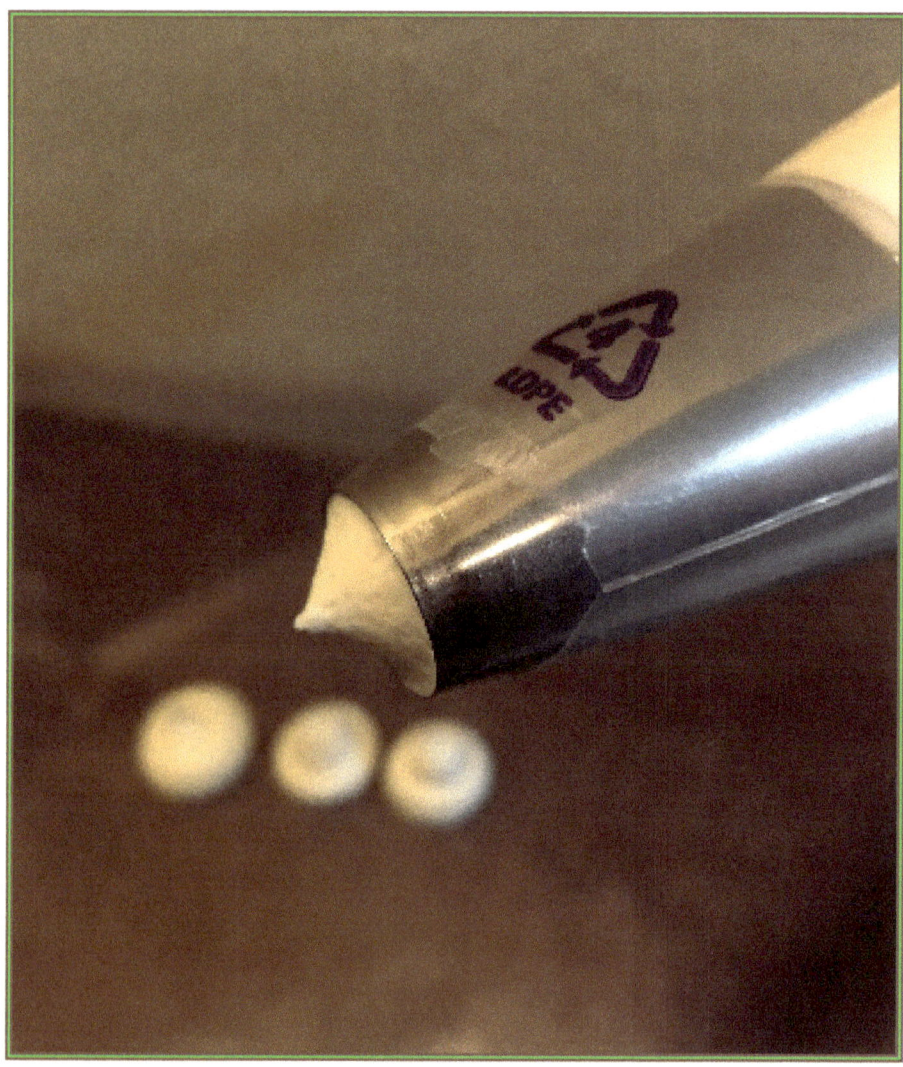

Rose Geranium Chocolate Pound Cake

Makes 1 (8-inch) Ring Cake

The Victorian era was witness to a number of botanical manias (for example, pteridomania, or "fern fever"). The herbal equivalent of this was the love of scented geraniums, which at the time could be found in hundreds of varieties (from musk or pine to violet or peppermint). But the most favored was the rose-scented geranium. Many a Victorian home cook would store a few rose geranium leaves in their sugar jar.

This era also saw the advent of baking scented geranium leaves into cakes, both to provide a subtle flavor and to create beautiful edible patterns and decorations. I used a ring pan here because I like the way the leaves wilt over the top of the cake, decorating the side and the top with a single leaf, but this could be baked in a loaf pan. If you have a hard time getting the leaves to stick to the side of the pan, simply lay them on top of the batter.

8-12 rose scented geranium leaves
¼ cup unsweetened cocoa powder
2 tablespoons boiling water
2 teaspoons Rose Water (see page 148)
1 ½ cups cake flour
1 teaspoon baking powder
½ teaspoon salt
1 cup butter, room temperature
1 cup rose geranium-Scented Sugar (see page 148)
3 eggs, at room temperature
1 ½ teaspoons vanilla
¼ teaspoon nutmeg, freshly ground)

Preheat oven to 350°. Grease and flour an 8-inch tube pan. Line the bottom of the pan with parchment paper. Use a dot of butter to glue the rose geranium leaves to the side of the pan.

In a small bowl, whisk the cocoa powder into the boiling water until smooth. Let the mixture cool to room temperature.

In a medium bowl, sift the cake flour together with the baking powder and salt.

In the bowl of a mixer, cream the butter and the sugar together until light and fluffy. Add the eggs one at a time, beating well after each addition. Add the vanilla, the rose water, and the cocoa mixture. Stir until well incorporated. Add the flour and mix until just combined.

Pour the batter carefully into the prepared pan, disturbing the geranium leaves as little as possible. Bake for 50-55 minutes or until a toothpick inserted in the center comes out clean.

Remove the cake from the oven and place on a wire rack to cool for about 10 minutes. Remove the cake from the pan, reinvert, and cool completely on a wire rack.

Herbie Info Box

Scented geraniums would more correctly be called scented Pelargoniums, as they actually belong to this genus. This is somewhat confusing, because Geranium is the name of a completely different genus, sometimes called cranesbills. To make things even more confusing, Pelargoniums are sometimes known as storksbills. They do all belong to the same botanical family.

Scented geraniums – as, following tradition, we will continue to call them – originate from Africa. Keeping that in mind, it is no surprise that they are heat-loving, drought-tolerant evergreens. However, they don't do well with frosts, so in climates with hard winters, most people either grow them in containers or plant them in beds for the summer and then dig them up and move them to a protected place to overwinter.

These plants are thought to have arrived in England in the 1600s aboard ships returning from visits to the Cape of Good Hope. It is there that they received their name. In 1738, Johannes Burman derived the name from pelargos, the Greek word for stork, as the seed head reminded him of a stork's bill.

Violet Chocolate Cheesecake
Makes 1 (9-inch) Cheesecake

Violets were popular both as a cut flower and as an ingredient in candies, gum, and perfumes in the eighteenth and nineteenth centuries. Fondness for these sweet blooms was fueled in part by Napoleon's declaration that the violet was his favorite flower. They were often used for creating little arrangements to top boxes of chocolates that gentlemen presented to their favored ladies. So we thought: Why not include the flavor of the violets in the chocolate? Their fleeting fragrance (violets give off a chemical that temporarily disables the sense of smell) will fill your kitchen during baking. Reinforce the violet's flavor profile by adding a little of the violet syrup to lemonade or sparkling water and serving it alongside the cheesecake. Remember to use only sweet violets or related scented violets (not African violets) for this recipe.

Cheesecake:
8 ounces bittersweet chocolate, chopped
¾ cup Violet Syrup (see page 149)
1 ½ cups chocolate mini grahams, crushed
3 tablespoons sugar
3 tablespoons butter, melted
24 ounces cream cheese, softened
1 ½ teaspoons vanilla extract
3 tablespoons flour
3 eggs
½ cup sour cream
1 cup sweet violet flowers, for garnishs

Preheat the oven to 350°. Line the bottom and sides of a 9-inch springform pan with parchment paper.

Combine the chocolate and the violet syrup in a double boiler over barely simmering water. Stir frequently until the chocolate melts and the mixture becomes smooth. Set aside and allow to cool.

In a large bowl, combine the crushed grahams, sugar, and butter and mix until uniform. Press the graham mixture onto the bottom of the prepared springform pan. Set aside.

In the bowl of a mixer, combine the cream cheese, vanilla extract, flour, eggs and sour cream. Beat until well combined. Add the melted chocolate mixture and beat until incorporated.

 Pour the batter on top of the graham mixture in the prepared springform pan. Bake for 1 hour or until the center is almost set. Run a sharp knife around the rim of the pan, and allow the cheesecake to cool completely on a wire rack before removing the collar of the pan. Refrigerate overnight before serving. Serve topped with fresh or candied violets.

Chocolate Pear Tart with Herbed Sweet Dough Crust

Makes 1 (10-inch) Tart

Choose firm, fully ripe pears for poaching. You want a variety that can stand up to the poaching process without becoming mushy or falling apart. Bosc pears are our favorite for this purpose. If you have to buy commercial pears, they will most likely have been picked before they were properly ripe. You can allow them to ripen on the counter for several days.

While there are a number of herbs included in this recipe, consider parsley. There are two main types of parsley that are grown for their leaves (some parsley is grown for the root, which can be carrot-shaped, or for the stalks, which can be a bit like celery). The "leaf" parsleys can be divided by flat leaf or curly leaf types. The curly leaf variety is certainly more impressive (and suitable for making garnishes), but the flat is considered more flavorful.

1 egg
1 cup sugar
¼ cup milk
½ cup butter
¼ teaspoon baking powder
2 cups flour, plus extra as needed
¼ cup fresh flat-leaf parsley, minced
1 tablespoon fresh basil, minced
2 teaspoons fresh oregano leaves, minced
2 teaspoons fresh thyme leaves, minced
1 batch Chocolate Custard (see page 125)
1 batch Poached Pears (see page 125)

Grease a 10-inch tart pan.

In the bowl of a mixer, cream together the butter and sugar. Add the egg and milk and mix on medium-low until incorporated. Then mix in the baking powder and flour. The dough should be sticky and elastic but should release from your hand. Add additional flour if necessary. Work in the fresh herbs, then roll the dough out onto a sheet of waxed paper to ¼-inch thick and transfer to a tart pan. Place in the freezer for at least half an hour.

When ready to proceed, preheat the oven to 375°. Remove the prepared tart pan from the freezer. Slice each poached pear half into arcs, slicing across the width of the pear, keeping the slices lined up in the original shape. Use a spatula to transfer each pear half into the tart shell, forming a circle of pears, with all the narrow ends pointing in. Fan the pears by pressing gently on the wide end to tilt them towards the narrow end.

Carefully pour the custard around the pears, leaving as much of the fruit as possible visible. Bake 50 minutes to an hour or until the custard is firm to the touch. Cool on a wire rack for 10 minutes.

Remove the tart from the tart pan and slide onto a serving dish. Serve warm.

Chocolate Custard

6 ounces bittersweet chocolate, chopped
¾ cup heavy cream
¼ cup sugar
2 eggs
1 teaspoon vanilla

Combine the chocolate, cream, and sugar in a double boiler over barely simmering water, stirring and folding the mixture until it is shiny and smooth. Set aside to cool.

Combine the eggs and vanilla in a large bowl and whisk until well combined. Temper the eggs by drizzling around a cup of the chocolate mixture to them, a little at a time, while whisking constantly. Add the rest of the chocolate mixture to the egg mixture, whisking until well incorporated.

Poached Pears

Poached Pears
4 Bosc pears, peeled, halved, and cored
5 cups water
1 cup vanilla-Scented Sugar (see page 145)
3 bay leaves
3 star anise
½ vanilla bean, seeds and pod

Combine the water, sugar, bay leaves, star anise, and vanilla in a large saucepan over medium heat, stirring constantly until the sugar has dissolved. Add the pears to the sugar mixture (adding additional water, if needed, to keep the pears fully covered) and reduce the heat to medium-low. Cook for 10-15 minutes or until the pears are fork tender. Strain the pears from the liquid and place into a medium bowl to cool. Discard cooking liquid.

Jasmine Liqueur Chocoflan
Makes 1 (Fluted Tube Pan) Cake

Chocoflan does a really cool trick in the oven: the layers switch places. You line the bottom of the pan with your chocolate sauce (for more of a color contrast, you could use a more traditional caramel), scoop in the cake batter, and then pour on the flan. Somehow, the cake floats to the top to become the cake base when you flip it. We added jasmine liquor to the flan mixture, because its delicate floral nature goes well with the creaminess of the milk. In lieu of jasmine, you could use a fennel or anise liqueur.

10 tablespoons butter, at room temperature, plus additional for greasing
3 tablespoons blond chocolate, melted
1 tablespoon water
1 cup sugar
1 egg, at room temperature
1 ¾ cups all-purpose flour
¾ teaspoon baking powder
¾ teaspoon baking soda
¼ teaspoon salt
⅓ cup cocoa powder
1 ¼ cups buttermilk
8 ounces evaporated milk
1 (14-ounce) can sweetened condensed milk
4 eggs
½ cup jasmine liquor
1 tablespoon vanilla extract

Preheat oven to 350°.

Combine the melted blond chocolate and water. Stir until smooth. Grease a fluted tube pan generously with butter, then coat the inside bottom of the pan with the blond chocolate sauce.

For the cake:
In a large bowl, whisk together the flour, baking powder, baking soda, salt, and cocoa. Set aside.

In the bowl of a mixer, cream the butter and sugar. Beat in the egg. Add ⅓ of the flour mixture and ½ of the buttermilk to the egg mixture and beat until smooth. Repeat, ending with the flour mixture. Blend until well incorporated.

For the flan:
In a blender, combine the evaporated milk, condensed milk, jasmine liquor, cream cheese, eggs, and vanilla. Blend on high for 30 seconds.

To assemble:
Scoop the cake batter into the prepared fluted tube pan and spread evenly. Slowly pour the flan mixture over the cake batter.
Prepare a water bath by using a baking sheet with a lip that can hold the fluted tube pan and ½-inch of water.

After sliding the pan into the oven, add the water to the pan and bake 1 hour, until the surface of the cake is firm to the touch or a toothpick inserted in it comes out clean. When the cake is done, remove it from the water bath and cool completely to room temperature (about 1 hour).

Place a serving plate upside down over the fluted tube pan. Hold them together, shake side to side a little to loosen the cake, and flip over.

Lemon Verbena Chocolate Crème Brulee

Makes 6 Servings

In the Victorian era, ladies often carried lemon verbena leaves in their handkerchiefs. They would hold these fragrant bundles to their faces and inhale deeply to refresh themselves when they felt fatigued. Modern aromatherapists concur with the Victorians, crediting lemon verbena with combating lethargy and lifting one's spirits. What a delightful herb to pair with chocolate! We also added a bit of pineapple sage to add further interest to the flavor. The caramel taste of the burned sugar adds yet another element. Garnish the finished crème brulees with whatever edible flowers are in season (we used petunias, along with the flowers from the pineapple sage). If you chill the custards overnight before bruleeing the sugar, moisture may form. Should this occur, very gently blot the surface of the custard with paper towels to remove any condensation.

You can use any small blowtorch if you don't have a brulee torch. Skip the caramelizing if you don't feel comfortable using a torch. Do not try to use your oven's broiler.

3 cups heavy cream
¾ cup turbinado sugar
⅛ teaspoon salt
25-30 lemon verbena leaves
8-10 pineapple sage leaves
6 large egg yolks
½ teaspoon vanilla
1 teaspoon lemon juice
¼ teaspoon lemon zest
2 ounces semisweet chocolate, finely chopped
6 teaspoons granulated sugar
6 pineapple sage flower clusters, for garnish
6 white petunias, for garnish

Preheat the oven to 300°.

In a small saucepan, bring the cream to a boil over medium heat, stirring occasionally. Stir in the Turbinado sugar and the salt. Remove the saucepan from the heat, and add the lemon verbena and pineapple sage leaves. Put the lid on the saucepan and allow the mixture to steep for half an hour.

Beat the egg yolks in a large bowl, then gradually strain the hot cream into them, whisking constantly. Stir in the vanilla and the lemon juice and zest. Add the unsweetened chocolate and whisk until it melts into specks.

Divide the mixture among six (6-ounce) ramekins. Arrange the ramekins in a pan and carefully pour water into the pan around them until it reaches approximately half the height of the ramekins. Bake for 30-35 minutes or until the custard is just set around the edges. Allow the custards to cool in the water bath for 20 minutes. Remove the ramekins from the pan, dry off the outsides, and chill, uncovered, at least 3 hours. Sprinkle about 1 teaspoon granulated sugar evenly over each custard, then caramelize the sugar using a brulee torch. Move the torch in an even motion back and forth close to the sugar until it melts into a solid plate. Garnish each ramekin with a petunia and a pineapple sage flower cluster.

Cocoa Masala Chai Soufflés

Makes 8 Servings

A cup of masala chai, creamy and perfectly spiced, is a warming treat perfect for a cold day. We get that same comforting warmth when biting into the delicate texture of a dessert soufflé. So here, we put the two experiences together, along with the richness of dark chocolate. In Kashmiri masala chai recipes, saffron often plays a part, so we topped these soufflés with a saffron cream sauce. Masala chai translates as: "mixed spice tea." (It is easy to shorten that to just "chai," but chai is simply the Hindi word for tea, so if you were to ask for that in India, you are just as likely to get a strong cup of plain black tea.)

You can prepare the soufflés up to the point of baking the day before you need to serve them. Just keep the ramekins well chilled until ready to bake.

8 cardamom pods
6 black peppercorns
2 cloves
1 (3-inch) cinnamon stick
½ teaspoon anise seeds
¼ teaspoon powdered ginger
⅔ cup milk
2 teaspoons black tea leaves
½ cup sugar, plus 3 tablespoons, divided, plus extra for sprinkling
2 tablespoons all-purpose flour
½ cup cocoa powder
2 egg yolks
1 teaspoon vanilla extract
4 large egg whites
⅛ teaspoon cream of tartar
3 ounces bittersweet chocolate, chopped
1 batch Saffron Cream Sauce (see page 131)

Preheat the oven to 375°.

Butter eight (6-ounce) ramekins. Sprinkle the inside of the cups with sugar, turning the cup as needed to completely coat the inside.

Place the cardamom pods, peppercorns, cloves, cinnamon stick, and anise seeds in a spice grinder and pulse until a powder is formed. Add the powdered ginger and set aside.

In a small saucepan over medium heat, combine the milk and the black tea leaves. Heat just until the mixture simmers, then remove the saucepan from the heat. Place the lid on the saucepan and allow the mixture to steep for 5-7 minutes. Strain out the tea leaves (discard solids).

In a small saucepan, combine the half cup sugar, flour, salt, and 3 tablespoons of the tea-milk. Stir to form a thick paste. Slowly add the remaining tea-milk in a steady stream, whisking constantly. Place the saucepan over medium heat and bring to a simmer. Stir constantly for 2-3 minutes or until the mixture begins to thicken. Remove the saucepan from the heat, and add the cocoa powder, cardamom spice mixture, egg yolks, and vanilla. Stir until completely incorporated.

In a separate large bowl, combine the egg whites and cream of tartar and beat until soft peaks form. Add the remaining 3 tablespoons of sugar, a little at a time, beating well between each addition. Continue beating the eggs until stiff peaks form. Add about a cup of the chocolate mixture to the egg mixture and carefully fold to combine. Add the remaining chocolate mixture, and fold until the two mixtures have been incorporated together. Fold in the chopped chocolate.

Pour the batter equally into the prepared ramekins, and place the ramekins on a baking sheet. Bake for 10-15 minutes or until the soufflés puff over the rim of the ramekins (a toothpick inserted in the soufflé should emerge with a layer of thick batter). Use a spoon to create a shallow depression in the top of each soufflé and fill it with a generous spoonful of the Saffron Cream. Serve immediately.

Saffron Cream Sauce

1 cup whipping cream
¼ cup powdered sugar
¼ teaspoon saffron strands

In a medium saucepan over medium-low heat, combine the heavy whipping cream, powdered sugar, saffron threads, and basil. Whisk constantly until the sugar is melted and the cream starts to simmer. Continue to simmer, stirring frequently, for 8-10 minutes or until the sauce has thickened. Remove from heat. Serve warm.

Espresso Tamarind White Chocolate Mousse with Clove Whipped Cream

Makes 8 Servings

Indonesia produces both chocolate and coffee, which share similar growing conditions. As of this writing, Indonesia is the fourth largest coffee producer in the world. Coffee, of course, is just one of Indonesia's many botanical exports. After all, what would you expect from a country that contains the Maluku Islands—better known as the Spice Islands. One of the spices native to the Malukus is clove, the dried flower bud of an Indonesian evergreen tree. Until recently, cloves were not grown anywhere else in the world. The profitable clove trade, carried out by ships heading towards all corners of the then-known world, was even mentioned in One Thousand and One Nights. This recipe celebrates the flavors of Indonesia, combined with distinctly European cooking techniques.

The tamarind adds quite a tang, so use the lesser amount if you have never tried it. The parsley/basil addition is not traditional, but we think it adds a refreshing element. Make sure the eggs are cooked to 160°, as that is considered the minimum safe temperature.

12 ounces white chocolate, chopped
½ cup espresso, plus ¼ cup, divided, at room temperature
1-1 ½ tablespoons tamarind paste
4 eggs, at room temperature
¼ cup vanilla-Scented Sugar (see page 148)
1 batch Clove Whipped Cream (see page 133)

In a double boiler over barely simmering water, combine the white chocolate and the ½ cup of espresso, whisking frequently until melted and smooth. Remove from the heat and whisk in the tamarind paste. Set aside to cool, but leave the water on the heat.

In a heatproof bowl, whisk the eggs with the vanilla sugar and the remaining ¼ cup of espresso. Set the bowl on top of the simmering water and cook, stirring constantly, until the egg mixture reaches 160°. Remove the bowl from the heat, and beat the egg mixture until soft peaks form (around four minutes).

Fold approximately one cup of the egg mixture into the chocolate mixture, then gently fold the egg mixture back into the chocolate mixture until completely incorporated. Carefully pour the mousse into eight ½ cup dessert dishes. Refrigerate the mousse for at least two hours or until well chilled. Immediately before serving, spoon a generous dollop of the cream on top of each chilled mousse and garnish with a grating of nutmeg.

Clove Whipped Cream

1 cup whipping cream
¼ cup powdered sugar
¼ teaspoon saffron strands

In a medium saucepan over medium-low heat, combine the heavy whipping cream, powdered sugar, saffron threads, and basil. Whisk constantly until the sugar is melted and the cream starts to simmer. Continue to simmer, stirring frequently, for 8-10 minutes or until the sauce has thickened. Remove from heat. Serve warm.

Herbie Info Box

Tamarind is a sticky, sweet fruit that grows in pods on a tropical tree. Tasting the fresh fruit off the tree is quite an experience. If you live where fresh or dried tamarind can be purchased, tamarind paste can easily be made by separating the pulp from the seeds and outer shell and cooking it with a little water until soft. Then it is simply mashed. It can be kept in the refrigerator for up to two months.

Truffles and Candy

In this Chapter you will find:

Gingered Ginseng Fudge

Hawaii-Inspired Mendiants

Rosemary Caramel-Filled Chocolates

Crystalized Ginger and Lemongrass Truffles

Pistachio and Cardamom Bark

Gingered Ginseng Fudge
Makes 1 (8 x 8-inch) Pan

China is a major world producer of walnuts, so walnuts seemed a natural choice to pair with ginseng in this fudge. There are 11 species of ginseng in the genus Panax (from the same Greek root as panacea). The part of the plant most often used is the root, although sometimes the leaves are included as well. Look for ginseng extract at the health food or vitamin store. The ginger syrup rounds out the flavor.

3 tablespoons butter, plus extra for greasing
1 cup walnuts, chopped
2 ¾ cups sugar
4 ounces unsweetened chocolate
¾ cup evaporated milk
¼ cup ginseng extract
1 tablespoon ginger-Simple Syrup (see page 151)
1 tablespoon vanilla

Grease an 8 x 8-inch pan.

Preheat the oven to 450°. Spread the walnuts on a baking sheet and toast for 5-8 minutes or until lightly browned. Set aside to cool.

In a medium saucepan, combine the sugar, chocolate, evaporated milk, ginseng extract, and ginger syrup over medium heat. Stir frequently with a wooden spoon until the sugar melts and the chocolate becomes smooth. Increase the heat to medium high, and bring the mixture just to a boil. Reduce the heat to medium-low, cover, and allow to boil for 3-4 minutes to let the sugar crystals wash down the sides. Remove the cover and continue stirring frequently until the mixture reaches the soft ball stage (234°).

Remove the saucepan from the heat and, without stirring, add the butter and vanilla. Let the mixture stand for eight minutes, then mix completely with the wooden spoon. Add the toasted nuts and continue mixing just until the chocolate mixture loses its gloss. Immediately pour into the prepared pan. Set the pan in a cool, dry area and allow the fudge to become completely solid before cutting into squares.

Hawaii-Inspired Mendiants

Makes 16 Pieces

Mendiants once featured only raisins, figs, almonds and hazelnuts (which represented the colors of monastic robes of orders common in France at the time mendiants were invented). However, modern confectioners have taken the round patty form and used it to highlight other ingredients. Rather than presenting the traditional "four beggars," we wanted to showcase four flavors of Hawaii, which has, after all, been growing cacao since the late 1800s (it is the only U.S. state with the necessary climate for doing so). Oranges aren't native to Hawaii either, but they grow so well there that they are sometimes thought by visitors as being indigenous, so we included a strip of candied peel. Of herbs grown commercially in Hawaii, parsley is second only to basil, and the candied bit of it reminds us of the lush greenness of the islands. And, of course, one must include macadamia nuts.

8 ounces milk chocolate, tempered (see page 17)
16 macadamia nuts
16 Candied Parsley Pieces (see page 146)
16 Candied Orange Peel Strips (see page 146)
16 Candied Pineapple Chunks (see page 147)

Line two baking sheets with parchment paper.

Transfer the tempered chocolate to a pastry bag fitted with a round tip, and pipe half a dozen ¾-inch diameter patties across the parchment paper. Top each patty with one macadamia nut, one candied parsley piece, one candied pineapple chunk and one candied orange peel strip. Repeat with the remaining chocolate, piping a half dozen patties at a time to prevent them from drying before they can be topped. Allow the mendiants to set completely before serving.

Rosemary Caramel-Filled Chocolates

Makes 2 Dozen Pieces

Shakespeare's doomed Ophelia says, "There's rosemary, that's for remembrance; pray, love remember..." The Bard based this speech on folk knowledge about plants, but recent studies have suggested that the scent of rosemary can actually improve memory and cognitive function. In the Victorian era, the language of flowers branded rosemary as a symbol of loyalty and fidelity, making it a token of love and an adornment at weddings. That's why we've chosen a heart-shaped mold for these caramels. Of course, feel free to craft the candies in whatever shape is most pleasing to you.

**1 ⅔ cups heavy cream
4 rosemary sprigs
2 cups sugar
2 tablespoons butter
40 ounces bittersweet chocolate, tempered
(see page 17)**

Place the heavy cream and the rosemary sprigs in a medium saucepan over medium heat. Bring the mixture just to a simmer, stirring occasionally, then remove the saucepan from the heat. Place a cover on it, and allow the cream to steep for at least 30 minutes. Strain out the rosemary sprigs (discarding solids).

Place the sugar in the bottom of a large Dutch oven over medium heat. Shake once to even out the sugar layer but do not stir. Watch closely until the sugar at the edge melts, then begin stirring the liquid sugar from the edge towards the middle. Continue stirring in this manner until all the sugar has melted. Stir constantly until the sugar turns a deep amber color.

Remove the saucepan from the heat, and (wearing a mitt to protect your hand) immediately whisk in half a cup of the cream. Whisk constantly as you add the remaining cream in a slow, steady stream. Add the butter and whisk until incorporated. Set the caramel sauce aside to cool.

Carefully spoon the chocolate into the candy molds, filling each well completely. Knock the mold against the counter to remove any bubbles, then set on the counter for about 5 minutes. Quickly flip the mold back over the bowl, letting most of the chocolate drain out. Place the mold right side up on the counter and use a flat scraper to remove the chocolate in between the individual wells. Refrigerate the mold for at least ten minutes or until set.

Transfer the caramel sauce to a pastry bag fitted with a round tip. Fill each of the chocolate-lined wells ⅔ of the way with the caramel. Refrigerate for at least 10 minutes or until set.

Transfer the remaining tempered chocolate to a pastry bag fitted with a round tip. Carefully pipe a layer of chocolate across the top of the mold, making sure you seal all the edges. Return the mold to the refrigerator and allow to set completely. Carefully unmold the chocolates.

Crystalized Ginger and Lemongrass Truffles

Makes 5 Dozen Pieces

Ginger is a relative of turmeric, cardamom, and galangal. Like turmeric and galangal, the part of the plant people eat is the rhizome. Crystalizing a ginger rhizome (usually labeled "gingerroot" at the store) brings out its spiciness, transforming it into a unique sweet that is delicious on its own. If you can find young, fresh ginger, it is easy to crystalize it yourself. If you can only find the more fibrous, mature ginger, skip it and buy the pre-crystalized bagged product.

The lemongrass here rounds out the flavor and grounds the Thai influence. It can be unpleasant to bite into lemongrass (even when cooked, it has a noticeable grittiness), so take the time to grind it as finely as you can. If you are not fond of heat in your chocolate, you can omit the dried chilies, but they do add a fruity note to the combined flavors.

¼ cup cocoa nibs
2 tablespoons sugar
3 stalks lemongrass, thinly sliced
6 dried bird's eye chilies
½ cup cocoa powder
2-inch finger of fresh ginger
20 ounces bittersweet chocolate
1 cup heavy whipping cream
½ cup Crystallized Ginger, finely diced (see page 147)
3 tablespoons honey
1 tablespoon vanilla

Preheat the oven to 250°. Spread the cocoa nibs on a separate baking sheet and toast for 15-17 minutes or until fragrant. Allow to cool. Grind together the cocoa nibs, sugar, and lemongrass in a mortar and pestle until it forms a smooth paste. Set aside.

Grind the dried chilies to a fine powder using a mortar and pestle. Transfer to a shallow bowl and add half of the cocoa powder. Whisk to combine. Set aside. Place the remaining cocoa powder in a separate shallow bowl.

Combine the cream and the fresh ginger in a medium saucepan over medium-high heat. Bring the mixture just to a boil, then reduce the heat to medium-low and simmer for five minutes. Strain the liquid into a large bowl (discard solids). Add the chocolate and stir and fold until the chocolate melts and becomes smooth.

Add the cocoa nib paste, crystallized ginger, honey, and vanilla. Combine until the mixture becomes uniform. Cover the bowl with plastic wrap and refrigerate for two hours or until the truffle mixture becomes hard enough to scoop. Scoop out 1-inch balls, rolling with your hands to smooth the edges. Place the truffles on a lined baking sheet, and place in the refrigerator for about half an hour.

Meanwhile, melt the unsweetened chocolate in a double boiler over just-simmering water.

One at a time, roll the truffles in the cocoa powder, then roll again in the cocoa powder and chili mixture and place in a single layer on a serving platter. Refrigerate for 20 minutes before serving.

Herbie Info Box

Lemongrass can withstand a freeze if it isn't too hard or long -- but it needs to be prepared first. To overwinter your lemongrass, trim it down to a height of about six inches shortly before the first scheduled frost. Mulch it heavily with bark. Fortunately, lemongrass grows in clumps, which keeps the middle more protected. So even if the outer shoots die from a frost, the middle usually survives.

Herbie Info Box

Ginger is one of those plants that is easy to grow from food scraps. If you have leftover ginger, soak it in water overnight, then plant it directly into the ground. This works especially well if the piece is sprouting or has growth buds. It shouldn't be long before the ginger puts up shoots. Give the plant about four months to get established before you disturb it, but after that you should be able to carefully harvest little bits from the sides. Avoid planting ginger in direct sun, water-logged soil, or anywhere it will be exposed to strong winds.

Pistachio and Cardamom Bark
Makes Around 20 Pieces

When you look at a pile of chocolate bark, it really does look a bit like tree bark, with jagged edges and variations in texture. Yet for all its rustic appearance, chocolate bark is still considered a chocolate bar (albeit, in its simplest form). True chocolate barks are composed of layers of multiple types of chocolate. They actually bear little resemblance to substances you see labeled "bark" in the baking aisle of the grocery store (which do not actually contain cocoa butter and are therefore not chocolate at all). Many sources claim that chocolate bark was an invention of chocolatiers who needed to use up tempered chocolate left over from making other confections.

The flavors here are inspired by India. We love cardamom. The plant is a member of the ginger family, but instead of being cultivated for the rhizome, it is grown for the seed pod. Though the plant is native to India, it has long found favor in other parts of the globe. Some sources state that the ancient Egyptians chewed cardamom pods to freshen their breath and clean their teeth and that the Romans used it to make perfumes. If you prefer, you can process the whole pods in a spice grinder to use in place of the cardamom seeds in this recipe. Alternately, the seeds should be removed from their pods just before you use them, as they lose their flavor quickly after being exposed to air.

8 ounces bittersweet chocolate, tempered (see page 17)
¼ cup dried cherries, finely minced
8 ounces white chocolate, tempered (see page 17)
¼ teaspoon saffron strands
½ teaspoon cardamom seeds, crushed
⅛ teaspoon pink Himalayan salt
1 ½ teaspoons dried rose petals
¼ cup salted pistachios, roughly chopped

Line a rimmed baking sheet with parchment paper. Stir the cherries into the tempered bittersweet chocolate. Pour the bittersweet chocolate onto the baking sheet and spread evenly with a spatula (it may not go all the way to the edge). Place the baking sheet in the refrigerator for at least ten minutes or until set.

Stir the saffron strands into the tempered white chocolate. Pour the white chocolate over the bittersweet chocolate layer and smooth it with a spatula. Quickly sprinkle on the cardamom seeds, rose petals, pistachios, and pink Himalayan salt. Allow to set completely, then break into pieces.

Pastes, Sugars, Dressings and Syrups

Here's a handy group of recipes you can use on their own, as well as in specific recipes from other chapters of this book. Think of it as a tool kit for basic herb preparations. In these applications, you can replace the specific herb and make, for instance, basil infused butter, or thyme-infused honey. Practice the techniques, and you will be able to riff on them with ease.

In this Chapter you will find:

Lemongrass-Infused Butter	**Rose Water**
Basil Paste	**Scented Sugar**
Cocoa Butter Pesto	**Violet Syrup**
Chocolate Balsamic Vinaigrette	**Candied Parsley**
Maraschino Cherries	**Candied Orange Peel**
Chocolate Balsamic Strawberries	**Candied Pineapple**
Strawberry Balsamic Syrup	**Herbal Simple Syrup**
Basil Orange Syrup	**Crystalized Ginger**
Lavender-Infused Honey	

Lemongrass-Infused Butter

**2 stalks fresh lemongrass
1 cup butter
2 teaspoons lemon zest**

Trim and discard tough tops and root ends from the lemon grass. Remove and discard the tough outer layers.

Cut each stalk lengthwise in half and cut into 2-inch pieces.

Place the butter in a saucepan and add the lemongrass pieces. Over high heat, melt the butter. When butter is melted, turn heat to low and stir often until flavors are blended, approximately 15-20 minutes. With a slotted spoon, lift out and discard the lemon grass. Strain the butter into a bowl. Add the lemon zest. Let cool, cover, and chill until solid.

Basil Paste

**2 cups basil leaves
¼ cup olive oil**

Place the basil leaves in a blender. Open the small hole at the top of the blender lid. Slowly drizzle in the oil as you pulse, until the leaves become finely chopped and you achieve a uniform paste. Transfer the mixture to a clean jar, and add a little more oil to cover and preserve the paste. Refrigerate until needed.

Cocoa Butter Pesto

**1 tablespoons pine nuts
1 clove garlic
½ cup fresh basil leaves, hard packed
2 tablespoons fresh parsley, hard packed
2 tablespoons Parmesan cheese, grated
5 tablespoon cocoa butter, melted and allowed to cool**

In a dry skillet over medium heat, toast the pine nuts. Allow to cool, then place along with the basil, parsley, Parmesan and cocoa butter in a personal-size blender cup. Puree until smooth.

Chocolate Balsamic Vinaigrette

¼ cup chocolate-infused balsamic vinegar
2 teaspoons dark brown sugar
1 tablespoon honey mustard
1 tablespoon fresh basil, minced
1 tablespoon garlic, chopped
½ teaspoon salt
½ teaspoon black pepper
¾ cup olive oil

Whisk together the chocolate balsamic vinegar, brown sugar, honey mustard, basil, garlic, salt, pepper and olive oil..

Maraschino Cherries

¾ c. granulated sugar
¾ c. ginseng green tea (prepared)
¼ c. lemon juice
1 cinnamon stick
½ tsp. freshly grated nutmeg
1 tbsp. vanilla extract
1 ½ lb. sweet cherries, pitted
1 ½ c. Maraschino liqueur

In a large pot over medium-high heat, combine the sugar, ginseng green tea, lemon juice, cinnamon stick, nutmeg and vanilla. Bring the mixture to a boil, the reduce the heat to medium-low. Add the cherries and simmer for around 7 minutes. Remove from the heat and stir in the Maraschino liqueur. Store in the refrigerator for at least a week before eating.

Chocolate Balsamic Strawberries

16 ounces fresh strawberries, hulled and sliced
¼ cup chocolate-infused balsamic vinegar
¼ cup sugar
½ teaspoon black pepper

Place strawberries in a bowl. Drizzle vinegar over strawberries and sprinkle with sugar and pepper. Stir gently to combine. Cover and let sit at room temperature for at least 1 hour.

Strawberry Balsamic Syrup

**1 cup fresh strawberries, hulled and sliced
¾ cup sugar
1 ½ tablespoons balsamic vinegar
1 ½ tablespoons water
½ teaspoon cracked black pepper**

In a small saucepan, combine the strawberries, sugar, balsamic vinegar, water, and pepper over medium high heat. Bring the mixture to a boil, stirring frequently. Reduce the heat to medium-low and simmer the mixture for 15 minutes. Skim any foam as it forms. Remove pan from heat and transfer to a serving container. Serve warm.

Basil Orange Syrup

**½ cup sugar
¼ cup water
1 teaspoon orange zest
½ cup freshly squeezed orange juice
2 teaspoons cornstarch
1 tablespoon butter
1 teaspoon Basil Paste (see page 145)**

Combine the sugar, orange zest, and water in a small saucepan over medium heat. Stir frequently until the sugar dissolves. Meanwhile, whisk the cornstarch into the orange juice. Pour the juice mixture into the sugar mixture. Bring the mixture back to a simmer, then cook until the syrup becomes thick (about ten minutes). Remove the saucepan from the heat. Add the butter and whisk until it is incorporated. Transfer to a decorative container. Serve warm.

Lavender-Infused Honey

**1 ¾ cups honey
¼ cup lavender flowers**

Combine the honey and the lavender flowers in a sterilized pint jar. Screw on the lid, shake, and set the jar in a sunny windowsill. Once a day for two weeks, flip the jar upside down and shake the contents. At the end of the two weeks, strain out the lavender flowers.

Rose Water

2 cups rose petals
Water
Ice

Place a clean brick in the bottom of a deep stockpot. Surround the brick with rose petals and add enough water to cover all the petals. (The water should not come more than halfway up the side of the brick.) Place a wide, shallow bowl on top of the brick. Bring the rose petal mixture to a boil, then reduce to a simmer.

Fill a large metal bowl (large enough to seal the edges of the stockpot) with ice. Place the large bowl on top of the stockpot, and allow the mixture to simmer for 3 to 4 hours, replacing ice as needed.

Turn off the heat, discarding remaining ice from the large bowl. Remove the shallow bowl from on top of the brick. Skim off the rose oil (reserving for another use) and pour the rose water in a clean container with an airtight lid. Allow to cool completely before lidding.

Scented Sugar

3 cups sugar
6 rose geranium leaves or 3 vanilla beans or other herb

Pour the sugar into a quart glass jar. Bury the geranium leaves or vanilla beans in the sugar. Place the jar in a cool, dry place and shake once a day for three weeks. Sift out the plant material (discard or reserve for another use).

Violet Syrup

**1 cup sweet violet flowers
1 cup water
2 cups sugar**

In a medium saucepan over medium high heat, combine the sweet violets and the water. Bring just to a simmer. Remove from the heat and place the lid on the saucepan. Allow the sweet violets to steep overnight. The next day, skim out the flowers (discarding solids). Add the sugar and place the saucepan over medium heat. Bring to a boil, stirring frequently until the sugar melts. Continue to cook, stirring occasionally until the syrup thickens (about ten minutes). Set aside to cool.

Candied Parsley

**1 large sprig parsley
¼ cup sugar
¼ cup water**

Place a large piece of waxed paper on the counter. Remove the individual leaves from the sprig of parsley. Discard the stem and set the leaves aside.

Combine the sugar and water in a small saucepan over medium heat. Cook, stirring constantly until the sugar melts. Add the parsley and lower the heat. Simmer until the syrup becomes very thick and turns a light amber color. Remove the leaves from the syrup and place on the waxed paper, ensuring that the pieces are not touching. Allow to dry completely.

Candied Orange Peel

**1 large orange
½ cup sugar
½ cup water**

Place a large piece of waxed paper on the counter. Quarter the orange and cut the orange flesh and part of the pith away from the peel of each piece. Square up the edges of each piece of orange peel for uniform thickness. Cut the pieces into strips.

Combine the sugar and water in a small saucepan over medium heat. Cook, stirring constantly until the sugar melts. Add the orange peel and lower the heat. Simmer until the syrup becomes very thick and the peel starts to turn translucent. Remove the peel from the syrup and place on the waxed paper, ensuring that the pieces are not touching. Allow to dry completely.

Candied Pineapple

**1 thick slice fresh pineapple, peel and core removed, diced
½ cup sugar
½ cup water**

Place a large piece of waxed paper on the counter.

Combine the sugar and water in a small saucepan over medium heat. Cook, stirring constantly until the sugar melts. Add the pineapple and lower the heat. Simmer until the syrup becomes very thick and the pineapple pieces take on a translucent look. Remove the pineapple from the syrup and place on the waxed paper, ensuring that the pieces are not touching. Allow to dry completely.

Herbal Simple Syrup

2-inch finger of ginger or 2 tablespoons lavender, fennel or other herbs, peeled and roughly chopped
¼ cup water
½ cup sugar

Combine all ingredients in a medium saucepan over medium heat. Bring to a simmer, then lower the heat and cook, stirring frequently until the syrup thickens (about 6-8 minutes). Remove from the heat. Strain out the ginger pieces (discard or reserve for another use). Set aside to cool.

Crystalized Ginger

1 cup fresh young ginger root, peeled and diced
3 cups water
1 cup sugar

Place a piece of waxed paper on the counter.

Combine the ginger and water in a large saucepan over medium-high heat. Bring to a simmer and cook for about half an hour or until the ginger is tender. Remove the saucepan from the heat. Strain the ginger (reserving the liquid) and return the ginger pieces to the saucepan. Add the sugar and ¼ cup of the liquid, and bring the mixture to a boil over medium heat. Cook, stirring frequently, until the syrup has almost evaporated and the sugar clinging to the pieces looks dry. Transfer the ginger pieces to the waxed paper, making sure that the pieces are not touching each other. Allow to dry completely.

Index

A
achiote 19
allspice 19, 65
almonds 65, 66, 136
anise 19, 67, 125, 126, 130, 131
apple cider vinegar 39, 62, 81

B
basil 28, 35, 42, 43, 49, 52, 53, 59, 76, 77, 79, 83, 95, 123, 131, 132, 133, 136, 145, 146
bay 69, 70, 71, 99, 125
bell pepper 31, 46, 47
bird's eye chilies 139
bittersweet chocolate 10, 20, 53, 65, 68, 69, 83, 86, 97, 100, 109, 111, 112, 121, 125, 130, 137, 139, 143

C
canella 19
cardamom 130, 131, 139, 142, 143
cayenne pepper 19, 38
celery seeds 62
cherries 114, 115, 143
chiles cascabel 65
chilies mulatos 65
chilies pasillas 65
chili powder 62, 69
chocolate-infused balsamic vinegar 28, 146
chocolate mint 95, 96, 105, 111
cilantro 31, 44, 45, 62, 63, 68, 69, 73, 108
cinnamon 19, 62, 65, 95, 99, 105, 110, 116, 117, 130, 131
cloves 28, 29, 37, 38, 40, 44, 45, 59, 60, 62, 65, 66, 69, 71, 130, 131, 132
cocoa butter 10, 11, 14, 28, 33, 34, 46, 47, 142, 145
cocoa nibs 13, 26, 40, 57, 99, 106, 139
cocoa powder 11, 14, 21, 32, 43, 49, 51, 55, 59, 62, 74, 75, 78, 93, 100, 114, 116, 118, 126, 130, 131, 139, 140
cumin 38, 39, 62, 73

D
dark chocolate 10, 13, 14, 17, 35, 37, 44, 73, 88, 97, 107, 114, 130

E
epazote 19, 44, 45

F
fennel 18, 21, 93

G
garlic 28, 29, 37, 38, 39, 40, 44, 45, 48, 59, 60, 61, 62, 65, 66, 69, 71, 79, 112, 145, 146
geranium 118, 119, 148
ginger 38, 39, 62, 110, 111, 112, 130, 131, 135, 139, 140, 141, 142, 151
ginseng 135
grapefruit zest 109

H
hibiscus flowers 26
honey 19, 32, 48, 49, 80, 88, 89, 90, 94, 97, 110, 139, 140, 146, 147

K
kaffir lime leaves 108

L
lavender 18, 20, 83, 97, 98, 103, 106, 107, 147
lemongrass 38, 39, 102, 103, 116, 117, 139, 140, 145
lemon thyme 25, 100
lemon verbena 67, 128, 129
lemon zest 29, 55, 60, 91, 106, 107, 128, 145

M
macadamia 91, 92, 136
marjoram 35, 40, 65, 67, 83
mascarpone cheese 76
matcha 95, 96
mexican oregano 65, 67
milk chocolate 10, 11, 14, 17, 25, 80, 91, 136
molasses 81, 110
mozzarella 28, 35, 36

N
nutmeg 79, 91, 92, 118, 133

O
orange peel 110, 136, 150
orange zest 25, 110, 111, 112, 147
oregano 19, 29, 35, 59, 65, 66, 67, 74, 79, 123

P
papaya 49
paprika 59, 62
parmesan cheese 37, 40, 48, 74, 75, 79, 145
parsley 29, 33, 37, 40, 60, 70, 71, 72, 76, 77, 79, 108, 123, 132, 136, 145, 149
peanuts 65, 66, 102, 103, 111
pineapple sage 128, 129
pine nuts 40, 52, 53, 145
pistachios 143
plantain 65, 66
porcini mushrooms 37
portobello mushrooms 37

R
raisins 65, 66, 136
red rooibos 26
rose 118, 119, 148
rosebuds 20
rosemary 35, 41, 50, 51, 79, 88, 137
rose petals 143, 148

S
saffron 130, 131, 133, 143
sage 35, 43, 57, 74, 83, 87, 90, 100, 101, 128, 129
savory 83, 87
semisweet chocolate 10, 93, 114, 115, 128
sesame seeds 65, 66
soy sauce 38, 39
stone ground chocolate 11
sweet violets 121, 149

T
tamarind 132, 133
tarragon 41, 54, 55
thyme 25, 35, 37, 65, 66, 70, 71, 79, 83, 91, 92, 100, 109, 123
truffle oil 37

U
unsweetened chocolate 10, 14, 71, 73, 81, 111, 112, 129, 135, 140
unsweetened cocoa powder 118

V
vanilla 14, 19, 20, 51, 93, 100, 101, 105, 111, 112, 116, 118, 119, 121, 122, 125, 126, 127, 128, 129, 130, 131, 132, 133, 135, 139, 140, 148

W
walnuts 90, 135
white chocolate 11, 17, 29, 30, 38, 39, 90, 95, 96, 102, 103, 108, 132, 133, 143, 157
white petunias 128

About the Authors

Amber Royer is a science fiction author whose work often veers into culinary territory. The protagonist of her Chocoverse series is a culinary arts student in a world where chocolate is the galaxy's most sought-after delicacy. The first book in the series, Free Chocolate, received favorable reviews from Publisher's Weekly and the Barnes-and-Noble-Sci-Fi-&-Fantasy-Blog. Book two, Pure Chocolate, will be released in March 2019. Royer maintains an author Instagram feed that focuses on tea, coffee, chocolate, and writing prompts. She has started making it a point to frequent local tea and coffee shops when she visits a new city, which has given her the opportunity to speak with small business owners and industry professionals. She has taught creative writing and nonfiction writing classes at UT Arlington for over a decade. One of her more popular classes is Writing Your Own Cookbook: From Heirloom to Fundraiser. She has self-published two cookbooks (including the original edition of this one) and had a column at Dave's Garden for several years.

Website:
    amberroyer.com
Instagram:
    amberroyerauthor
Twitter:
    @amber_royer
Pinterest:
    https://www.pinterest.com/dandylyon85/
Facebook:
    Business Page – https://www.facebook.com/Dandylyons Garden-254236964650677/
    Author Page – https://www.facebook.com/Amber.Royer.Author/
YouTube:
    https://bit.ly/2Mn2Yws

Jake Royer, civil engineering designer by day, urban gardener by weekend, began his love of chocolate at an early age. Although his taste for fine chocolate has been developed by sampling single-source chocolates at the Dallas Chocolate Festival and other spectacular chocolate creations he has encountered along the way, he still harbors a not-so-secret love of Oreos. He has always been fascinated by how things work and loves to take food back a step from the finished product to the raw materials. Why buy yogurt (or herbal syrup or glacé fruit) when you can make it even better? He is also the pastry chef of the family and the green thumb. He has been gardening for over 20 years and has a semi-regular blog. As an artist, his favorite materials are glass, wool, and wood. He also loves taking pictures, and he and Amber often stop on the side of the road or pull into a parking lot when he spots an unusual plant he wants to photograph.

Website:
   gardentimeline.blogspot.com
Instagram:
   vachtra
Twitter:
   @vachtra

You can visit the home page for their small business, **Dandylyon's Garden**, at *dandylyonsgarden.com* or her writing site at *amberroyer.com*.

www.ingramcontent.com/pod-product-compliance
Lightning Source LLC
Chambersburg PA
CBHW051600010526
44118CB00023B/2761